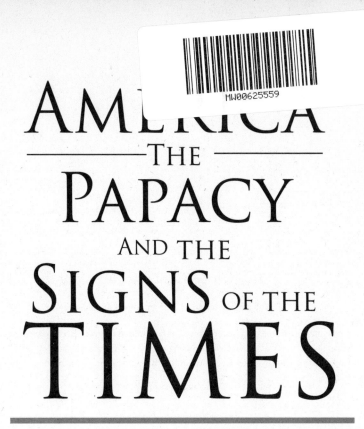

AMERICA
—— THE ——
PAPACY
AND THE
SIGNS OF THE
TIMES

A.L. DUNCAN / E.G. WHITE

EDITED BY OLSON PERRY

ISBN 978-0-9749490-3-1

Library of Congress Control Number: 2015912138

Printed in the United States of America

Published by Advent Truth Ministries, Inc. Forsyth, GA 31029
www.adventtruth.org

ABOUT THIS BOOK

*I*n these records we may see a foreshadowing of the conflict before us. Regarding them in the light of God's Word, and by the illumination of His Spirit, we may see unveiled the devices of the wicked one, and the dangers which they must shun who would be found "without fault" before the Lord at His coming. The great events which have marked the progress of reform in past ages are matters of history, well known and universally acknowledged by the Protestant world; they are facts which none can gainsay. This history I have presented briefly, in accordance with the scope of the book, and the brevity which must necessarily be observed, the facts having been condensed into as little space as seemed consistent with a proper understanding of their application. In some cases where a historian has so grouped together events as to afford, in brief, a comprehensive view of the subject, or has summarized details in a convenient manner, his words have been quoted; but in some instances no specific credit has been given, since the quotations are not given for the purpose of citing that writer as authority, but because his statement affords a ready and forcible presentation of the subject. In narrating the experience and views of those carrying forward the work of reform in our own time, similar use has been made of their published works.

It is not so much the object of this book to present new truths concerning the struggles of former times, as to bring out facts and principles which have a bearing on coming events. Yet viewed as a part of the controversy between the forces of light and darkness, all these records of the past are seen to have a new significance; and through them a light is cast upon the future, illumining the pathway of those who, like the reformers of past ages, will be called, even at the peril of all earthly good, to witness "for the word of God, and for the testimony of Jesus Christ."

To unfold the scenes of the great controversy between truth and error; to reveal the wiles of Satan, and the means by which he may be successfully resisted; to present a satisfactory solution of the great problem of evil, shedding such a light upon the origin and the final disposition of sin as to make fully manifest the justice and benevolence of God in all His dealings with His creatures; and to show the holy, unchanging nature of His law, is the object of this book. That through its influence souls may be delivered from the power of darkness, and become "partakers of the inheritance of the saints in light," to the praise of Him who loved us, and gave Himself for us, is the earnest prayer of the writer.

E.G.W.

PREFACE

The first seven chapters of this book are contributed by Aubrey L. Duncan of Advent Truth Ministries. They are intended to give the reader a simple, yet systematic, Bible study on the prophesies of Daniel and the Revelation as they relate to the events that are now coming to pass in these closing scenes of earth's history. These prophesies, as presented in this volume, testify to the veracity and dependability of God's Word to all humanity, the Holy Bible.

People everywhere are wondering about where the world is headed. Interweaving history, prophecy, and contemporary world affairs, this volume offers some intriguingly fascinating and compelling answers to questions confronting the human family today.

The reader is encouraged to prayerfully study the prophesied events, compare them with the historical record, and evaluate them in the light of contemporary world affairs. The honest heart would have to conclude that the hand of Omnipotence is indeed indelibly involved in the affairs of men.

The final eight chapters are adopted from the classic, the Great Controversy. Its author, Ellen G. White, was recently cited as one of the ten most influential religious leaders of all time by the prestigious Smithsonian Magazine. In her book, written more than one hundred years ago, she vividly discusses and portrays today's world affairs in a most succinct and remarkable way.

My sincere prayer is that you will not only be blessed, but that you will be drawn closer to our Lord and Savior, Jesus Christ, and thus be prepared for what is coming upon this world as an overwhelming surprise. It is my sincere prayer that this book will help you get prepared for that soon coming crisis and be ready to meet Jesus when He comes.

A.L.D

TABLE OF
CONTENTS

CHAPTER 1

The Signs of the Times

*I*n November of 1994, a landmark document was completed and signed by leading Roman Catholics and prominent Evangelical 'Protestants'. It was well publicized both in the secular and religious media. The initiative was hailed across denominational lines as a new beginning of cooperation between Catholics and Protestants. The document, entitled Evangelicals and Catholics Together (ECT), sought to bring together the many Christian factions into one communion of the body of Christ under the aegis of the church of Rome. The very thought that such a document could be conceived a few decades ago is incomprehensible. Oh, but how far have we come. Who would have imagined that such a proposition would not only be possible; but would be endorsed by a wide cross section of Christian leaders and accepted by multitudes of Christians.

Journalist, minister, and author, Chris Hedges, characterizes this movement thus: This movement is a hybrid of fundamentalists, Pentecostals, Southern Baptists, Conservative Catholics, Charismatics, and other evangelicals, all of whom are at war doctrinally, but who nonetheless share a belief that America is destined to become a Christian nation, led by Christian men who are in turn directed by God.... Lately the leaders of the movement have even begun to reach out to Mormons. America becomes, in this militant Biblicism, an agent of God, and all political and intellectual opponents of America's Christian leaders are viewed, quite simply, as agents of Satan.

From a Biblical perspective, one would only have to read and understand the 13th and 17th chapters of Revelation to grasp the significance of such a development. Scripture foretells that such attempts at unity between Roman Catholics and professed Christians would take place on the threshold of Jesus' return.

According to Scripture, this conglomeration of religious entities, along with world political powers, will not be for the good of society; but rather for the persecution of God's true followers. John the Revelator foretells, "And the ten horns which thou sawest are ten kings, which have received no kingdom as yet; but receive power as kings one hour with the beast. These have one mind, and shall give their power and strength unto the beast. These shall make war with the Lamb, and the Lamb shall overcome them: for he is Lord of lords, and King of kings: and they that are with him are called, and chosen, and faithful (Revelation 17:12-14).

In defining the unity which this document seeks to achieve, the Roman Catholic Apostle's Creed was quoted. This creed recites the belief of all adherents to the efficacy of the Roman Catholic Church as the only means of salvation for all believers. All who sign this document, therefore, subscribe to this belief. Herein lies the great problem for those who seek salvation through the only One who can give it, Jesus Christ. This is a grave dilemma in which Bible-believing Christians, who support this and other similar accords, find themselves. The Manhattan Declaration, a subsequent and much stronger initiative, calls for unity of the several faiths in taking political action to uphold and enforce their dogmas in order to save society from moral declension.

The Scriptures are abundantly clear. Our Savior declares, "I am the Way, the Truth and the Life. No one cometh unto the Father but by Me" (John 14:6). The apostle Peter, no doubt believing what his Savior had taught, exclaimed to his Jewish brethren, "Neither is there salvation in any other; for there is none other name under heaven given among men whereby we must be saved" (Acts 4:12). Jesus never engaged in political action or petitioned the state for enforcement of His teachings. He reached men's/women's hearts, one at a time with unspeakable love.

Only one of these positions can be true; either salvation through Jesus Christ or through political action and the sacraments and practices of Roman Catholicism. They are mutually irreconcilable. The ECT, Manhattan Declaration, and other such initiatives, designed to bring unity and change society for the better, will in fact have the opposite effect—disunity, chaos, and ultimately, tyranny. Such is the nature and history of church/state union. Rather than being led by God's Holy Spirit, whom ironically these initiatives invoke, they are fueled by the Papacy's grand strategy for world domination.

The signatories to these documents consistently call for unity among Catholics and Protestants in the name of Jesus Christ. This is a grave deception. The prophet Amos asks us, "Can two walk together except they agree" (Amos 3:3). The apostle Paul admonishes Christian believers, "Be ye not unequally yoked with unbelievers. For what fellowship hath righteousness with unrighteousness and what communion hath light with darkness" (2 Corinthians 6:14). How then can these documents or any attempt at unity between Roman Catholicism and Protestantism be the will of God, as they all claim?

Catholicism by its very nature, teachings and doctrines is contrary to the Christian faith. Whatever common ground it finds with Christianity is not patently Christian at all. Rather, commonality can only be found in some basic moral values professed by almost all mankind, religious and non-religious alike. This is indeed a good thing. It is upon this notion that the ECT and other Roman Catholic initiatives at 'church' unity are built. But here ends the similarity between Christianity and Catholicism.

Beyond these core human values, Catholicism differs from Christianity as night differs from day. Those differences gave rise to the Protestant Reformation. Protestantism grew out of the belief that men and women are to seek God and salvation according to the dictates of their own consciences, and not the dogmas of the Catholic Church. Hence, the word, "Protestant." Having come to the light of God's Word, men and women began protesting against the unbiblical teachings of the 'church,' none of which have been renounced by her.

As we look across the religious landscape today and peruse documents like ECT and Manhattan Declaration, one is forced to ask the question, where are the Protestants? Who would have believed that the Lutheran Church, founded by the most famous Protestant Reformer, Martin Luther, would find its way back to Rome? The idea of Protestantism was born in that period of earth's history termed the Dark Ages. It was thus called because the Roman Catholic Church, as she ruled the world, (538AD-1798AD) made it her first order of business to keep the Word of God away from the people. God's Word teaches, "Thy word is a lamp unto my feet and a light unto my path" (Psalms 119:105). Since the Light was taken away, then there was only darkness left. Historian Wiley declared that the noonday of the papal reign was the midnight of the world. In the place of God's Word, a plethora of pagan doctrines, church traditions, and ecclesiastical dogmas were instituted. Although many of them continue today with Christian names and connotations, their essential falsity still remains. A prime example is Sunday sacredness which was adopted in the place of God's holy Sabbath-day.

Could Martin Luther and the other Protestant Reformers see from their graves, they would be appalled at how the nations of the world and the Protestant churches are clamoring back to Rome. They would be mystified at how, in a day when the Bible is freely and readily available, men are turning from the light of God's word to the traditions of the Roman Church. Ironically, the same Evangelicals who are so readily seeking unity and cooperation with the Roman Church, are now calling for the return of the nations to God's Ten Commandments law.

This is indeed a glorious discovery on their part which places them in a great dilemma; particularly in light of the fact that almost all of them have, and vigorously continue to teach that God's law was nailed to the cross at the crucifixion of Jesus Christ. As such, they proclaim that we do not have to keep the law.

It is not only ironic, but somewhat puzzling to see these leaders in this position. They proclaim, rather confidently, that we are not under law but under grace and therefore do not have to keep the law. They continue to parrot that the law was only for the Jews. Now that the chickens have come home to roost, they are attempting to come together in an elusive unity to appeal to the state to enforce their beliefs. Perhaps, Benjamin Franklin's warning needs to be heeded: "When religion is good, it will take care of itself. When it is not able to take care of itself, and God does not see fit to take care of it, so that it has to appeal to the civil power for support, it is evidence to my mind that its cause is a bad one" (Letter to Dr. Richard Price, October 19th, 1790).

For those, like the Seventh-day Adventists, who have insisted that God's law is eternal and must be kept by all men in all times, the labels of legalist and works salvation have been branded upon them. Nevertheless, the Seventh-day Adventists and other Sabbath Keeping Christians, building their faith on the Bible alone, have always taught and practiced that God's moral law, which includes

His Sabbath commandment, is binding upon all men for all times. My question is, what do you call the zealous Evangelicals who now are willing to go to prison in order to have the Ten Commandments placed in the public square and are petitioning the state to enforce them? Perhaps they need to be reminded that it is not on tables of stone, but in their hearts that God's law must be written.

In fact, their very name 'Evangelical' would appear to be a grave oxymoron. For the word Evangelical is derived from the term evangelist, one who preaches the Gospel of salvation by God's grace through faith in His Son, Jesus Christ. One would be hard pressed to find any Biblical Evangelist appealing to state powers to enforce their teachings.

May God be praised for the awakening of these individuals. Their discovery had led them to come together under the banner of the Ten Commandments Commission. Ron Wexler, the first chairman of this auspicious commission, made this appeal, "At a time when the Ten commandments are being banned from the public places, along with prayer, Scripture and expressions of faith, it is crucial for people of faith from all walks of life to take a bold stand for righteousness… that is what the Ten Commandments Commission is all about… to enable people to come together in unity and declare their commitment to God's holiness and righteousness".

This amazing discovery of the evangelical world demands a concerted decision with regard to the Sabbath commandment which reads, "Remember the Sabbath day, to keep it holy. Six days shalt thou labour, and do all thy work: But the seventh day is the Sabbath of the Lord thy God: in it thou shalt not do any work, thou, nor thy son, nor thy daughter, thy manservant, nor thy maidservant, nor thy cattle, nor thy stranger that is within thy gates: For in six days the Lord made heaven and earth, the sea, and all that in them is, and rested the seventh day: wherefore the Lord blessed the Sabbath day, and hallowed it. (Exodus 20:8-11).

Their decision to uplift God's Ten Commandments as the moral foundation of the nation is a noble one. However, it creates a self-inflicted dilemma. God's holy law, which they are rightfully bringing to men's attention, explicitly states that His Sabbath is the seventh day of the week, today called Saturday. Nevertheless, almost the entire Christian world observes Sunday, the first day of the week, as the Sabbath. Now that they have discovered the efficacy God's Ten

Commandments, the question is, whose Sabbath will they honor? Will it be that of the God of creation, or will it be that of man's tradition. This is a decision every Christian will personally have to make.

Ellen G. White, the world renowned nineteenth/twentieth century Christian commentator whom the Smithsonian Magazine recently named of the top 10 religious leaders in American history, writes rather prophetically, "The Sabbath will be the great test of loyalty, for it is the point of truth especially controverted. When the final test shall be brought to bear upon men, then the line of distinction will be drawn between those who serve God and those who do not. While the observance of the false Sabbath in compliance with the law of the state, contrary to the fourth commandment, will be an avowal of allegiance to a power that is in opposition to God, the keeping of the true Sabbath, in obedience to God's law, is an evidence of loyalty to the Creator. While one class, by accepting the sign of submission to earthly powers, receive the mark of the beast, the other, choosing the token of allegiance to divine authority, receives the seal of God" (Great Controversy, Ellen G. White, page 605).

She further warns God's people, "The Romish Church now presents a fair front to the world, covering with apologies her record of horrible cruelties. She has clothed herself in Christ-like garments; but she is unchanged. Every principle of popery that existed in past ages exists today. The doctrines devised in the darkest ages are still held. Let none deceive themselves. The popery that Protestants are now so ready to honor is the same that ruled the world in the days of the Reformation, when men of God stood up, at the peril of their lives, to expose her iniquity. She possesses the same pride and arrogant assumption that she lorded over kings and princes, and claimed the prerogatives of God. Her spirit is no less cruel and despotic now than when she crushed out human liberty, and slew the saints of the Most High" (ibid, page 570).

As the Evangelicals continue their rapid march back to Rome, it is this writer's sincere prayer that the scales be removed from their eyes and they will indeed turn to see Jesus, the Author and Finisher of their faith and the Only Shelter in the coming storm.

CHAPTER 2

The Enemy in the Camp

*I*n his very insightful, and in many ways, prophetic volume, Keys of this Blood, Jesuit scholar and Vatican expert, Malachi Martin, talked about the three way competition for world domination. He identified the players, whom he considered the only ones with the resources to engage in such a contest, as Capitalism, Communism, and Catholicism. He then concluded that ultimately there will be only one victor. Martin stated, "Nobody who is acquainted with the plans of these three rivals has any doubt but that only one of them can win. Each expects the other two to be overwhelmed and swallowed up in the coming maelstrom of change. That being the case, it would appear inescapable that their competition will end up as a confrontation" (The Keys of this Blood, pg. 15).

Since the publication of his book in 1990, one of those three players, Communism, has been effectively neutralized. The other two, Capitalism and Catholicism, had joined forces to bring about the demise of Communism in the former Soviet Union and Eastern Bloc nations. Today, even in other so-called Communist states, Capitalism remains the engine that drives their economic machinery. For all intents and purposes, there are only two players left of Malachi Martin's three—Capitalism and Catholicism, as epitomized by President Barak Obama and Pope Francis respectively.

Time Magazine of February 24, 1992 headlined the epic of Capitalism joining forces with Catholicism to defeat Communism. The magazine's cover glared this headline: HOLY ALLIANCE… How Reagan and the Pope conspired to assist Poland's Solidarity Movement and hastened the demise of Communism. The ensuing article, written by award-winning journalist, Carl Bernstein, detailed the actions of the Papacy and the United States in bringing about Communism's downfall.

However, since his appointment as the supreme head of the Papacy (Catholicism), some three years ago, Pope Francis has launched a frontal attack on Capitalism, decrying its evil influences on the human family and its destructive impact on the environment. Noted Columnist, Paul B. Farrell, made this eye opening observation in a commentary in Market Watch, "Pope Francis's target is clear: economic inequality is the world's No. 1 problem. Capitalism is at the center of all problems of inequality. And he speaks with a powerful moral authority — something totally missing from American political leaders who are ideologically guided by atheist Ayn Rand, patron saint of the GOP's capitalism agenda in this moral war. Without moral grounding, the GOP is no match for Francis' vision, his principled mandate, his long-game strategy to raise the world's billions out of poverty, to eliminate inequality, to attack the myopic capitalism driving today's economy, markets and political system".

Farrell continued, "Moreover, the pope has the resources: As commander-in-chief of the world's largest army: 1.2 billion Catholics worldwide who are now motivated to defeat capitalism's grip on inequality. His army includes 78 million Americans in 17,645 parishes, plus a huge officer corps of 213 cardinals, over 5,000 bishops, 450,000 priests and deacons worldwide, all sworn to carry out his vision. He needs no legislative approvals; popes have authority to act unilaterally, with speed, a dictator whose word is law, commanding allegiance, obedience and action" (Market Watch, November 18, 2014).

The Capitalist camp, of which the United States is undoubtedly the leader, is either totally oblivious or willingly ignorant of the fact that they are in a head on confrontation with Catholicism. The idea that the enemy is in the camp is a most untenable notion. As he prepared to welcome the pope to speak to the American people, President Barak Obama, the face of Capitalism and the epicenter of Universal Capitalism, expressed his admiration for the pope thus, "I welcome His Holiness Pope Francis's encyclical, and deeply admire the Pope's decision to make the case – clearly, powerfully, and with the full moral authority of his position – for action on global climate change". The president continued, "As Pope Francis so eloquently stated this morning, we have a profound responsibility to protect our children, and our children's children, from the damaging impacts of climate change...I look forward to discussing these issues with Pope Francis when he visits the White House in September. And as we prepare for global climate negotiations in Paris this December, it is my hope that all world leaders–and all God's children–will reflect on Pope Francis's call to come together to care for our common home". It is quite amazing to hear such words from an American president who is also a Constitutional scholar. He must not be aware of the roots of the American experience.

Nevertheless, not only is Francis vehemently attacking Capitalism, he is inciting a revolution against it as he casts himself as the champion of the poor whom he pictures as victims of that inhumane and immoral system. The great irony of this is that the pope had chosen Latin America, consisting of some of the poorest countries in the world, where his religion is the largest and is intimately entwined with the people and governments of that region, to launch his poverty revolt (New York Times, July 14, 2015).

Another remarkable irony is that Francis' Papacy is perhaps the largest beneficiary and supporter of Capitalism. Its investments in banking, real estate, transportation, and the Military/Industrial Complex, the bedrock of capitalism, is very well documented in the best-selling volume, Vatican Billions, by Avro Manhattan, an expert on Vatican financial affairs. Avro Manhattan concluded: "The Catholic Church, therefore, once all her assets have been put together, is the most formidable stockbroker in the world. The 'Wall Street Journal' said that the Vatican's financial deals in the U.S. alone were so big that very often it sold or bought gold in lots of a million or more dollars at one time. Therefore, the Vatican was, and still is, the most redoubtable wealth accumulator and property owner in existence. No one knows for certain how much the Catholic Church was, or is worth in terms of dollars and other currencies, not even the pope himself. That is the true situation borne out by a Vatican official who, when asked to make a guess at the Vatican's wealth today, replied very tellingly, "Only God knows" (Vatican Billions, Ch 26).

This being the case, and if Francis is truly concerned about the poor and disenfranchised, why don't he begin by divesting his papacy of some of its hoarded wealth to help remedy the situation?

To the casual, uninformed, and somewhat deceived observer, it appears that Pope Francis, as the visible head of Catholicism, is indeed a trailblazing champion of the poor and disenfranchised.

Viewed through those lenses, his attack on Capitalism may be justified. But when viewed through the prism of the grand chessboard of Geopolitics, a different picture emerges. As Francis advances his charge on Capitalism, he is strengthening his relationship with world leaders of all hues and contours. He is, at the same time, declaring that the Protestant Reformation is now over and urging the separated brethren (formerly heretics) to come back home. And they are answering the call en masse. Additionally, he has positioned himself as the most pious and influential of all religious leaders. Essentially, Francis is not only preparing to be the victor, but sees himself as the head of the One-World System of government, as Malachi Martin predicted, " that has ever existed in the society of nations".

Malachi Martin, with no reference to Bible prophecy, was verily elucidating what the God of Creation had revealed to His servant John, almost 2,000 years ago on the mount of Patmos. In the thirteenth chapter of the Book of Revelation, John foretells of the time in which the United States of America will join forces with the Roman Papacy, restoring it to its former position to which it aspires– yea is orchestrating, to rule the world (Revelation, chapter 13).

Dr. John Robins, in his book, Ecclesiastical Megalomania writes, "Ayn Rand was right when she wrote in 1967, 'The Catholic Church has never given up the hope to re-establish the medieval union of church and state with a global state and global theocracy as its ultimate goal'. The Roman church/state is a hybrid, a monster of ecclesiastical and political power. Its political thought is totalitarian and whenever it has had the opportunity to apply its principles, the result has been bloody repression. If during the last 30 years it has softened its assertions of full, supreme and irresponsible power and has murdered fewer people than before; such changes of behavior are not due to a change in its ideas but to a change in circumstances… it is only when the Roman church/state faced public opinion that disapproved of church/state sanctioned murder, that it slowed its persecutions and attempted to speak with a voice less bloodthirsty. The Roman church/state in the 20thcentury, however, is an institution recovering from a deadly wound. If and when it regains its full power and authority, it will impose a regime more sinister than any the planet has ever seen" (E. M, page 195). Considering its history of the Dark Ages, when tens of millions who disagreed with her policies were mercilessly slaughtered, Professor Robbins' assertion must not be taken lightly.

Ellen G. White, eloquent nineteenth century Bible commentator, is in total agreement with Professor Robins. She wrote in her classic, The Great Controversy, "Let the restraints now imposed by secular governments be removed and Rome be reinstated in her former power, and there would speedily be a revival of her tyranny and persecution" (Great Controversy, 564).

Top Vatican adviser, Jeffrey Sachs, wrote that when Pope Francis visits the United States, he will directly challenge the "American idea" of God-given rights embodied in the Declaration of Independence. Sachs, a special advisor to the United Nations and director of the Earth Institute at Columbia University, writes in the Jesuit publication, America, "[America] is a society in thrall" to the idea of unalienable rights to life, liberty, and the pursuit of happiness. But the "urgent core of Francis' message" will be to challenge this "American idea" by "proclaiming that the path to happiness lies not solely or mainly through the defense of rights but through the exercise of virtues, most notably justice and charity."(Western Journalism, May 19, 2015). To the discerning eye, it is clear that repudiating the American Constitution and substituting Papal dogmas in its place is Francis' ultimate objective, thus establishing itself as the leader of the New World Order and the victor in Malachi Martin's three way competition for world domination.

True to promise, Francis has done exactly as Sachs foretold. In the pope's address to the United States Congress on September 24th 2016, he unabashedly decried the evils of Capitalism and in effect proposed that a new model–Papal rule, be implemented in its place. His repeated refrain was that the state should unite with the church to solve humanity's problems; the church of course being the arbiter of what's right and what's wrong. Howard Fineman, Global Editorial Director of the Huffington Post, says it best in his article entitled, Pope Francis Wants To Be The President Of The World. He observes, "But shrewdly, methodically and with a showman's flair, the soft-spoken, 78-year-old Argentinian Jesuit priest named Jorge Mario Bergoglio — Pope Francis — showed Thursday that he is running to become president of the planet. He did so in a congressional ceremony of secular civic pomp in a massive legislative building that, after all, harks back to ancient Rome. As devout as he is, and as focused on the faith and practice of the Catholic Church, Francis is also campaigning to lead public, secular, political discourse worldwide. He is arguing that the two realms of faith and politics are one, and that the moral and spiritual teachings of faith should inform and guide political decisions for "our common home" (Huffington Post, September 26, 2015)

But statesman and patriot, the late Richard Thompson, Secretary of the Navy and author of The Papacy and the Civil Power, long ago remarked, "Nothing is plainer than that, if the principles of the Church of Rome prevail here, our constitution would necessarily fail. The two cannot exist together. They are in open and direct antagonism with the fundamental theory of our government and of all popular government everywhere." The late Charles Chiniquy, former Roman Catholic priest concurred with Robins, White and Thompson. He wrote, "The American Constitution assures the absolute independence of civil from the ecclesiastical or church power; but the Church of Rome declares, through all her pontiffs and Councils, that such independence is an impiety and a revolt against God" (Fifty Years in the Church of Rome, pg. 478). The leaders of America, mesmerized by Francis' presence coupled with the pomp and circumstance that attended his every move, applauded as he effectively ordered them to repudiate the U.S. Constitution with its solid foundation of separation of church and state.

The United States Congress, in its infancy, constructed its founding documents as bulwarks against Papal incursion and rule. It is indeed very sad to see, now in its maturity, a little more than two hundred years later, that body assuring the Papacy, the most dangerous foe of Civil and Religious Liberty, that it will follow its lead.

Though seemingly a happy marriage in the making, a confrontation (as indicated by Malachi Martin) between Capitalism and Catholicism, is inevitable. The two will indeed unite for a short period of time, for the purpose of persecuting those who oppose them; but will ultimately end up in a tectonic struggle of apocalyptic proportions. So says John the Revelator: "And he [America] had power to give life unto the image of the beast [Papacy], that the image of the beast should both speak, and cause that as many as would not worship the image of the beast should be killed. And he causeth all, both small and great, rich and poor, free and bond, to receive a mark in their right hand, or in their foreheads: And that no man might buy or sell, save he that had the mark, or the name of the beast, or the number of his name. (Revelation 13:15-17). And the ten horns

[10 World Divisions] which thou sawest are ten kings, which have received no kingdom as yet; but receive power as kings one hour with the beast [Papacy]. These have one mind, and shall give their power and strength unto the beast. These shall make war with the Lamb, and the Lamb shall overcome them: for he is Lord of lords, and King of kings: and they that are with him are called, and chosen, and faithful" (Revelation 17:12-14).

But finally, perhaps too late, they discover the enemy in the camp and then turn against her with vengeance and fury. John concludes, "And the ten horns which thou sawest upon the beast, these shall hate the whore, and shall make her desolate and naked, and shall eat her flesh, and burn her with fire. For God hath put in their hearts to fulfil his will, and to agree, and give their kingdom unto the beast, until the words of God shall be fulfilled. And the woman which thou sawest is that great city, which reigneth over the kings of the earth" (Revelation 17:16-18).

CHAPTER 3

The Push for Sunday Sacredness

ormer Pope Benedict XVI, not unlike his predecessors, was adamantly determined to advance his church's efforts for unity of all Christians. He exclaimed, "The commitment of the Catholic church to the search for Christian unity is irreversible" (USA Today, June 27th, 2005). That unity is rooted and grounded in Sunday sacredness. The love affair of Evangelicals and Catholics is truly a fulfillment of the Biblical prophecy of the whole world wandering after the beast (Revelation 13:3,8). In direct opposition to God's call to honor His true Sabbath (Exodus 20:8-11; Revelation 14:7) is the call to honor, and ultimately enforce Sunday as a universal day of rest. Sunday sacredness is the glue which unites Catholicism and not only almost all of Protestantism, but the rest of the religious world as well.

Newspapers and magazines are replete with articles on the need to honor and reverence Sunday as a day of rest. Time Magazine, featured this headline in an article calling for Sunday sacredness, "And on the Seventh Day We Rested? Maybe those old, blue laws weren't crazy after all" (Time, August 2, 2004). The article, written by Nancy Gibbs, one of the magazine's top columnists, went on to enunciate the sanctity of Sunday and heralded a call for the nation's return to honoring it as a sacred day. Similarly, the Sunday Times of London reported on the late Pope John Paul ll Encyclical Letter, Dies Domini (The Day of the Lord): "It is also expected to win support from other churches, particularly from Evangelical Christians, who share the Pope's anxiety about the erosion of the Sabbath" (The Sunday Times,

5 July, 2004). This is not referring to God's Sabbath; but rather to Rome's Sunday.

The Pope's strong appeal and stern exhortation to the world at the document's release was, "Make it clear that Sunday must not be worked, since it must be celebrated as the day of our Lord." Monsignor Miquel Delgado Galindo, Under Secretary for the Pontifical Council for the Laity, appealed to the faithful, "The church teaches us to set aside this day, the first day of the week on which we remember the resurrection of Jesus Christ, for divine worship and for rest.... On Sundays Catholics should participate in the Holy Mass, the un-bloody renewal of Christ's sacrifice on the cross and the greatest expression of worship and adoration that man can offer to the Lord our God" (Catholic News Service July 19, 2011).

This of course is contrary to the Word of God. The Creator calls us to rest on His blessed Sabbath day, the seventh day of the week, not the first. The question is, who are you following on the matter of God's Sabbath? Further, former Pope Benedict XVI sent out the call as he celebrated mass in Vienna, Austria in the year 2007. He insisted that Sunday must be protected as a day of worship. Zenith, the Papacy's official news agency reported the Pope's concern regarding the establishment of Sunday as a universal day of rest. Says he, "At a time when creation seems to be endangered in so many ways through human activity, we should consciously accept this dimension of Sunday, too...It is necessary to promote reflection and efforts at reconciling the demands and the periods of work with those of the family and to recover the true meaning of the feast, especially on Sunday, the weekly Easter, the day of the lord, and the day of man, the day of the family, of the community, and of solidarity" (Zenith. org, Sept. 26 2010).

Even in Jewish Jerusalem the movement for Sunday sacredness has taken root and growing exponentially. The following is simply mind boggling: "Sabbath-Sunday Bill-Survey shows support: MK Zevulun Orlev (NRP) has announced the findings of a poll showing 56 percent support for his proposed legislation making Sunday a day of rest and allowing some public transportation and entertainment on the Sabbath" (Israel National News Service, Hillel Fendel, May 31, 2007). The article went on to show the wide appeal of Zevulun Orlev's proposal. In presenting his proposal to the Knesset (Parliament), Orlev declared, "The idea's main purpose is to allow the religious and traditional public to use the day of rest to spend time with the family, something which is not possible for Shabbat observers" (ynetnews. com, 5/14/07).

The European Sunday Alliance was launched in Brussels on June 20th, 2011. It has as its theme: "Together for decent working hours." The organization which is comprised of several civil society organizations, trade unions, and churches has committed to ensuring legislation that will "commit to safeguard and promote work-free Sundays and decent working hours throughout Europe."

The National Back to Church Sunday movement is the largest cross-denominational outreach initiative in America. It is an organization that seeks to get more people returning to church on Sunday. Philip Nation, one of the organization's founding members remarked, "The enthusiasm for National Back to Church Sunday has grown along with the number of churches participating."

Lord's Day Alliance USA says: Sunday is a "MARK" of Christian Unity (April 2015). "By definition, each and every Sunday is a call to Christian unity since it is on this day that we are called to communion with the Lord, by the Lord ... In order to fully appreciate Sunday as a mark of Christian unity we must expand our definition of unity."

On March 27th, 2015, Sylvia Allen, a Republican Senator in Arizona commented on a new gun law to allow concealed carry permit holders to carry their guns into public buildings. Apparently, she thinks the new law is necessary because of the failure of all Americans to attend church on Sunday. Speaking of the "horrible erosion of the soul of America," Allen said, "We are slowly eroding religion at every opportunity we have... Probably we should be debating a bill requiring every American to attend a church of their choice on Sunday to see if we can get back to having a moral rebirth."

These initiatives appear quite innocent and beneficial on the surface. But there is an undercurrent of which very few are aware. Ellen G. White again warns God's people, "The Sunday movement is now making its way in darkness. The leaders are concealing the true issue, and many who unite in the movement do not themselves see whither the undercurrent is tending. Its professions are mild and apparently Christian, but when it shall speak it will reveal the spirit of the dragon" (Testimonies to the Church, vol. 5 page 452).

In his Encyclical Letter of July 2009, a copy of which was personally delivered to President Barak Obama, former Pope Benedict

XVI addresses the plethora of social, economic, environmental, and political problems that plague our world today. He then proposed his cure all solution: "In the present social and cultural context, where there is widespread tendency to relativize truth, practicing charity in truth helps people to understand that adhering to the values of Christianity is not merely useful but essential for building a good society and for true integral human development" (Charity In Truth, Section 4). The question is, to whose Christianity is he referring? He goes on to answer that question as he later proposes a social "order that confirms to the moral order." He is undoubtedly referring to the 'social' and 'moral' order as taught and practiced by his church. That social and moral order has as its foundation Sunday sacredness. What he offers to ensure adherence to 'the moral order' is most frightening. Benedict recommended the formation of a 'true world political authority vested with the power to ensure security and compliance' with his prescribed social and moral order. Essentially, Benedict is not only expressing his view for solving the world's problems, but letting everyone know that the only solution to those problems is a universal church/state union based on the moral values of his church. This is not only a frightening thought, but verily the fulfilling of John's vision of Revelation chapters 13 and 17—a world-wide religious/political order controlled by the church of Rome.

The current pope, Francis I, has not only continued the call for Sunday sacredness, but has captivated the entire world as he diligently seeks to unite all humanity under the rulership of the Papacy. The Associated Press recently reported: "Pope Francis lamented the abandoning of the traditionally Christian practice of not working on Sundays, saying it has a negative impact on families and friendships. … He says that spending Sundays with family and friends is an 'ethical choice' for faithful and non-faithful alike." He later added, "Preserving the special character of Sunday as the Lord's Day — even civilly where possible." As a Jesuit priest, Francis no doubt subscribes to the overarching objective of his order which is to return all "heretics" (separated brethren) back to the fold of the mother church. A cursory look at his movements since replacing Benedict, in a rather surprising and unusual course of events, bespeaks his success of bringing the "heretics" back home and thus uplifting Sunday sacredness.

➤ January 21, 2014-Appealed for Christian unity to a group of leading influential Evangelical leaders. He declared to them that," We are all Catholics now." The response to his appeal was heralded as a positive step in the right direction.

➤ March 13, 2014-The Speaker of the U.S. House of Representatives, Republican John Boehner, extended an invitation for Francis to address a full session of the United States Congress. Democrat Nancy Pelosi, a former Speaker of the House fully supported Boehner, indicating that she has been "inspired by the Pope's message of peace, compassion, and brotherhood". Francis of course accepted the historical invitation and addressed the nation on September 24, 2015. During his visit to the United States, he also addressed the United Nations and the World Meeting of Families in Philadelphia. One can hardly imagine the stomach-churning amazement of the Founding Fathers who established this nation as a bulwark against Papal incursion.

➤ March 27, 2014-Pope Francis met with President Barak Obama at the Vatican. The two discussed the need for solidarity in solving the world's problems.

➤ May 9, 2014-Francis advised the United Nations on solving the world's economic problems. His solution: "the legitimate redistribution of economic benefits by the state, as well as in indispensable cooperation between the private sector and civil society." Influential columnist, John Moody, wrote about this event, saying, "Francis…became what amounts to a robe-wearing politician."

➤ June 1, 2014-The Pope attended a gathering of 53, 000 Charismatics gathered in Rome for the 37th National Convention for the Renewal of the Spirit Conference.

➤ June 5, 2014-A fifteen person delegation, including mega church pastor, Joel Osteen and members of the Mormon Church met with the Pope to discuss the question: "Can we find common ground to advance the ministry of Jesus so more people can experience the joy of Christian faith?" Joel Osteen commented on the meeting, " I felt very honored and very humbled…I like the fact that this Pope is trying to make the church larger, not smaller… he is not pushing people out, but making the church more inclusive. That resonated with me."

➤ October 25, 2014-Jerry White, U.S. Deputy Assistant Secretary of State, called for a "global covenant of religions" with the Pope at the head. This came on the heels of Israeli president, Shimon Perez, calling for a United Religions organization citing the Pope as a central figure for world peace.

➤ On May 23rd, 2015 in Phoenix, Arizona, Francis addressed the John 17 Movement, an organization formed to bring Catholics and Evangelicals together. He reiterated his appeal for all to be reunited and come back to the mother church. He beckoned, "It is unity we are seeking along a common path. It is the unity of our common labor."

Additionally, the Pope travelled to the Holy Land visiting holy sites of Jews, Christians and Muslims. He subsequently invited the presidents of Israel and Palestine to the Vatican where they were joined by Christians, Jewish, and Islamic religious leaders to pray for peace.

Following a meeting with several U.S. televangelists, responding to his call for Christian unity, Francis established a Council to Promote Global Christian Unity. Leading American pastor, Rick Warren, after his meeting with the Pope, declared that Catholics and Protestants are on the same page.

Nevertheless, the Pope's declaration to a group of more than 30,000 Catholics should have awaken the sleeping saints to Francis' real objective. To this gathering on June 24th, 2014, Francis passionately announced, "There are those who believe that they can maintain a personal, direct and immediate relationship with Jesus Christ outside the communion and mediation of the church. THESE ARE DANGEROUS AND HARMFUL TEMPTATIONS." Thus was the policy of his church that led to the slaughter of tens of millions who chose to believe that salvation is available through Jesus Christ, and Him alone (John 14:6, Acts 4:12).

Clearly, the Roman Church, with Francis at its helm, believes that the solution to the world's economic, political, moral, and religious problems rests with her. The universal call for Sunday sacredness, Francis's church professed mark of authority in religious matters, is being presented to the masses as a time of rest from the stresses and bustle of everyday life. This was undoubtedly his appeal to the various audiences he addressed during his visit to the United States.

However, the ultimate objective of the prime mover behind the Sunday movement, the Church of Rome, is more dogmatic. We read these revealing words in Dies Domini, "When, through the centuries, she has made laws concerning Sunday rest, the Church has had in mind above all the work of servants and workers, certainly not because this work was any less worthy when compared to the spiritual requirements of Sunday observance, but rather because it needed greater regulation to lighten its burden and thus enable everyone to keep the Lord's Day holy. In this matter, my predecessor Pope Leo XIII in his Encyclical Rerum Novarum spoke of Sunday rest, as a worker's right which the State must guarantee (Dies Domini, Section 66).

In plain language, Rome is using the argument of rest to camouflage her real purpose of forcibly instituting Sunday sacredness, the mark of her authority, in the place of God's Holy Sabbath-day. But you need not be deceived. God has already given us a day of rest. The record reveals, "Thus the heavens and the earth were finished, and all the host of them. And on the seventh day God ended his work which he had made; and he rested on the seventh day from all his work which he had made. And God blessed the seventh day, and sanctified it: because that in it he had rested from all his work which God created and made." (Genesis 2:1-3). You do not need Rome's counterfeit. Besides, He does not force us to keep it; He lovingly beckons us to honor it.

Certainly, the call for Sunday rest as it is promoted to the public, is not so much about rest, but rather for the sacredness of Sunday, in blatant opposition to God's Seventh-day holy Sabbath. It is a call to show submission to the Pope of Rome. The establishment of universal Sunday sacredness is inevitable. This sampling of efforts to impose Sunday sacredness from around the world is but the prelude of what prophecy foretells will come to pass.

In times of tragedy and catastrophe, when there seems to be no other way out, men seek the help of God. September 11th, 2001 was one such occasion of national and international scope. Following that great tragedy, church attendance sky rocketed as people sought the help of God for understanding and finding solace from the unimaginable.

To many, this meant going to church on Sunday. No one knows when the next catastrophe will occur. Whether it be another terrorist attack, worldwide financial meltdown, some uncontrollable disease, natural disaster, or any combination thereof, one thing is for sure is that men will seek the help of God.

In such a time, the call for Sunday sacredness will fall on welcoming ears. Each will have to make a choice. The Roman church put forth a rather bold challenge to all Christians in a series of articles published in the year 1893 in the Catholic Mirror, the official organ of Cardinal Gibbons and the Papacy in the United States. It was then, and still is today, a matter of eternal consequences to every 'Protestants' who keep Sunday. Those articles, compiled into a booklet entitled, Rome's Challenge, states: "The arguments contained in this pamphlet are firmly grounded on the word of God, and having been closely studied with the Bible in hand, leave no escape for the conscientious Protestant except the abandonment of Sunday worship and the return to Saturday, commanded by their teacher, the Bible, or, unwilling to abandon the tradition of the Catholic Church, which enjoins the keeping of Sunday, and which they have accepted in direct opposition to their teacher, the Bible, consistently accept her in all her teachings. Reason and common sense demand the acceptance of one or the other of these alternatives; either Protestantism and the keeping of Saturday, or Catholicity and the keeping of Sunday. Compromise is impossible."

The apostle John foretells that even in this climate of deadly threats and far-reaching apostasy, God will have a faithful remnant; there will yet be Protestants. He prophesies, "And the dragon was wroth with the woman and went to make war with the remnant of her seed, which keep the commandments of God and have the testimony of Jesus Christ" (Revelation 12:17). Then he assures us, "These shall make war with the Lamb, and the Lamb shall overcome them: for He is Lord of Lords and King of Kings: and they that are with Him are called, and chosen, and faithful" (Revelation 17:13, 14). Which side of the battle are you on? Jesus assures us victory if we are on His side. By faith, you can and must choose the Lamb and be on His side by choosing His blesse Sabbath, thus rejecting Sunday sacredness, Rome's mark of authority.

CHAPTER 4

World History Foretold

The seal of God is His Holy Sabbath-day. It is the sign of authority within His law which identifies Him as its author. The Sabbath commandment reads, "Remember the Sabbath day, to keep it holy. Six days shalt thou labour, and do all thy work: But the seventh day is the Sabbath of the Lord thy God: in it thou shalt not do any work, thou, nor thy son, nor thy daughter, thy manservant, nor thy maidservant, nor thy cattle, nor thy stranger that is within thy gates: For in six days the Lord made heaven and earth, the sea, and all that in them is, and rested the seventh day: wherefore the Lord blessed the Sabbath day, and hallowed it" (Exodus 20:8-11).

God's name and His title are embodied within it. It specifies His sphere of authority. Further, it is the emblem of God's everlasting covenant relationship with all humanity. The Seventh-day Sabbath is God's sign between God and His people signifying that they belong to Him and are totally dependent upon Him for all their needs. Moses writes, "Six days may work be done; but in the seventh is the Sabbath of rest, holy to the Lord: whosoever doeth any work in the Sabbath day, he shall surely be put to death. Wherefore the children of Israel shall keep the Sabbath, to observe the Sabbath throughout their generations, for a perpetual covenant. It is a sign between me and the children of Israel for ever: for in six days the Lord made heaven and earth, and on the seventh day he rested, and was refreshed. And he gave unto Moses, when he had made an end of communing with him upon Mount Sinai, two tables of testimony, tables of stone, written with the finger of God. (Exodus 31:15-18).

The apostle Paul teaches that anyone who accepts Jesus Christ as their Lord and Savior becomes an Israelite. "For as many of you as have been baptized into Christ have put on Christ. There is neither Jew nor Greek, there is neither bond nor free, there is neither male nor female: for ye are all one in Christ Jesus. And if ye be Crist's, then are ye Abraham's seed, and heirs according to the promise" (Galatians 3:27-29). Being heirs of the promise also entails obligations to the commands. Therefore, in a very particular way, by faith, the Sabbath commandment, as the other nine, becomes obligatory upon the Christian.

However, the Bible refers to a power which, in the end of time, would have universal dominion over every nation, kindred, people and tongue. The prophet Daniel foretells that in addition to being a persecuting power, it would seek to set itself up above God by claiming to change God's law, particularly His Sabbath commandment. That power is referred to as 'the beast' (Daniel 7:25).

The Bible further teaches that the beast will have a 'mark' that will affect the survival of every person on planet earth. But who is the beast and what is its mark? More importantly, however, is the question of how the beast and its mark relate to God and His seal. Whatever they are, the beast and its mark are in contradiction to God and His seal of authority, His blessed Sabbath-day.

In the process of identifying and confirming what truly is 'the beast' and what is its 'mark', we will pinpoint its place in history as was prophesied in God's Holy Word almost 1000 years prior its rise in historical record. We will examine the part it is playing in contemporary world affairs. We will unlock the Biblical prophecies of the role of the beast and its mark in end time events. We will discover that God's holy Sabbath will be the issue most contested in the hearts and lives of men everywhere. This is becoming evident as the part played by the beast and its mark become more manifest.

Some say that the mark of the beast is a computer chip that would be implanted on the forehead or on the right hand of every inhabitant on planet earth. Others say that it will be some sort of smart card that would identify someone as being approved by the New World Order. That card, they say, will enable some to buy and sell when others can't. Surely, the technology is available or being developed that can accomplish those tasks. However, as people of faith, our only true answers must come directly from the Word of God. Whatever the beast and its mark is, the Bible admonishes us to be aware of them and, by God's grace, avoid them. The Bible makes it abundantly plain, that the consequences for receiving the mark of the beast are dire and deadly. John the Revelator warns, "And the third angel followed them saying with a loud voice 'If any man worship the beast and his image, and receive his mark in his forehead or in his hand, the same shall drink of the wine of the wrath of God, which is poured out without mixture into the cup of his indignation: and he shall be tormented with fire and brimstone in the presence of the holy angels, and in the presence of the Lamb" (Rev. 14:9-10).

John also predicts a most horrific consequence for those who receive the mark of the beast. He continues, "And the first (angel) went, and there fell a noisome and grievous sore upon men which had the mark of the beast, and upon them which worshipped his image" (Rev. 16:2).

In both of these accounts, John is referring to the last plagues that would be poured out upon the earth. They are not mixed with God's mercy. Grace is no longer pleading for the sinner. Man's probation is closed. Jesus has declared, "He that is unjust, let him be unjust still: and he which is filthy, let him be filthy still: and he that is righteous, let him be righteous still: and he that is holy, let him be holy still" (Rev. 22:11). Jesus makes His glorious return to planet earth to rescue and redeem the righteous, and to punish the wicked and disobedient. The harvest for His kingdom is ripe, and so is the harvest for the fires of hell. John further reports, "And the beast was taken, and with him the false prophet that wrought miracles before him with which he deceived them that had received the mark of the beast, and them that worshipped his image. These both were cast alive into the lake of fire burning with brimstone." (Revelation 19:20).

Quite interestingly, however, the beast does offer some benefits to those who receive his mark and worship his image. He threatens those who refuse his authority by choosing God's seal rather than receiving his mark. John describes the conflict, "And he had power to give life unto the image of the beast, that the image of the beast should both speak, and cause that as many as would not worship the image of the beast should be killed…And he causeth all, both small and great, rich and poor, free and bond, to receive a mark in their right hand, or in their foreheads: And no man might buy or sell, save that he had the mark, or the name of the beast, or the number of his name" (Rev 13:15-17).

Every human being on planet earth would have to make a choice. Either you would receive the seal of God; in which case you will suffer and perhaps die at the hand of the beast. Or, you will receive the mark of the beast, enjoy its benefits for a season, but then suffer the wrath of God as the plagues are poured out without mercy, and ultimately suffer eternal death. There is no middle ground. This is why it is vitally important that you know exactly, from the Word of God, what truly is the beast and what is its mark.

In order to determine what is the mark of the beast we must first identify what or who is the beast. For this we go to the word of God. It is the only reliable source for correctly identifying the beast and determining what is its mark. The prophet Daniel tells us what a beast is. In a vision, received from God whilst in Babylonian captivity, Daniel is shown the history of the world from his time down through the ages, unto the second coming of Jesus Christ. The nations, which will be successive, dominating world powers, were represented to Daniel as "beasts." Each would have a significant impact on God's people and His plan of redemption for men's souls. God's prophet relates, "These great beasts, which are four, are four kings, which shall arise out of the earth" (Daniel 7:17). He continues, "The fourth beast shall be the fourth kingdom upon the earth, which shall be diverse from all kingdoms, and shall devour the whole earth, and shall tread it down and break it into pieces" (Daniel 7:23).

God's servant not only tells us what a beast is, but gives us some identifying characteristics of 'the beast'. Clearly, Daniel is using a beast to denote a political power or nation. He further tells us that 'the beast' would at some time rule the entire earth with a policy of cruelty and fierceness. He gives us further insight: "Daniel spake and said, I saw in my vision by night, and behold the four winds of the heaven strove upon the great sea… and four great beasts came up from the sea diverse one from the other" (Daniel 7:2-3). The beasts we have already identified as political powers. Daniel says that winds of heaven strove upon the sea. And what are the winds and the sea? Isaiah answers: "Woe to the multitude of many people, which make a noise like the noise of the seas, and to the rushing of nations, that make a rushing like the rushing of mighty waters…The nations shall rush like the rushing of many: but God shall rebuke them, and they shall flee far off, and shall be chased as chaff of the mountains before the wind, and like a rolling thing before the whirlwind" (Isaiah 17:12-13).

Daniel, like Isaiah, is thus describing the warring and strife amongst nations as they struggle against each other for political and military domination. The first beast, or nation, that Daniel mentions is a lion with eagles' wings. He prophesies, "The first was like a lion and had eagles wings" (Daniel 7:4). In prophesying about Judah's captivity into Babylon, the prophet Jeremiah declared, "The lion is come up from ticket, and the destroyer of the Gentiles is on his way; he is gone forth from his place to make thy land desolate. And thy cities shall be laid waste without an inhabitant" (Jeremiah 4:7). He continues, "Behold he shall come up as clouds and his chariots shall be as a whirlwind: his horses are swifter than eagles. Woe unto us for we are spoiled" (Jeremiah 4:13). God's prophet makes it even clearer, "And this whole land shall be a desolation and an astonishment: and these nations shall serve the king of Babylon seventy years" (Jeremiah 25:11). The first beast of Daniel's dream identifies, unquestionably, the nation of Babylon into which he and the people of Israel were taken into captivity in the year 606 BC. Daniel then sees another beast (nation) coming at the first beast. "And behold another beast, a second like unto a bear" (Daniel 7:5).

The prophet Isaiah not only prophesied that God's people will go into captivity into Babylon; but that they will be liberated by the Persians. He records, "That saith of Cyrus, He is my shepherd, and shall perform all my pleasure: even saying to Jerusalem, thou shalt be built, and to the temple, thy foundation shall be laid. Thus saith the Lord to his anointed, to Cyrus, whose right hand I have holden, to subdue nations before him: and I will lose the loins of kings to open before him the two leaved gates: and the gates shall not be shut" (Isaiah 44:28, 45:1). Exactly as was prophesied, history testifies that Cyrus, king of Persia, conquered the kingdom of Babylon and granted the Jewish people their release from captivity in Babylon. Cyrus' emancipation decree allowed for the Israelites to return to Jerusalem and rebuild their temple.

The scribe Ezra reports, "Now in the first year of Cyrus king of Persia, that the word of the Lord by the mouth of Jeremiah might be fulfilled, the Lord stirred up the Spirit of Cyrus, king of Persia, that he made a proclamation throughout all his kingdom, and put it also in writing saying: Thus saith Cyrus, king of Persia: 'The Lord

God of heaven hath given me all the kingdoms of the earth: and he hath charged me to build Him an house at Jerusalem, which is at Judah" (Ezra 1:1-2). Cyrus, king of Persia, in his design to conquer the kingdom of Babylon, instructed his general Darius, to redirect the waters of the river Euphrates from its normal course which ran through the city of Babylon. The Euphrates, having been deferred from its normal flow thus leaving a hallow bed, allowed Darius' army to enter the Babylonian capital undetected. He entered the city beneath the gates on the dry land from where the river Euphrates was redirected. That act spelled the capture of Babylon by the Medes and the Persians.

Daniel records: "In that night was Belshazzar, the king of the Chaldeans slain and Darius the Median took the kingdom, being about three score and two years old" (Daniel 5:30, 31). The Medes were vassals of the Persians. Darius, the Median, was acting under the authority and direction of Cyrus, king of the Persians. It is thus clearly established that the second beast (nation) of Daniel's dream, represented by the bear, is none other than the empire of the Medes and Persians. History records that the year of the Persians capture of Babylon was 536 B.C., exactly 70 years after the captivity of the Israelites by the Babylonians. The prophetic utterances of both Isaiah and Jeremiah were perfectly realized.

Daniel's vision continues: "After this, I beheld, and lo another, like a leopard, which had upon the back of it four wings of a fowl: the beast had also four heads: and dominion was given to it" (Daniel 7:6). What nation was it that conquered the Media/Persian Empire? The historical record is undeniable. In the early half of 4th century B.C., the Grecian conqueror and ruler, Alexander the Great, made several incursions into the Media/Persian Empire. Finally, in the fall of 331 B.C., he defeated Darius III, king of the Persians at the Battle of Gaugamela (commonly referred to as the Battle of Arabela). This victory completed Alexander's conquest of the then known world.

Alexander the Great completed this feat at the tender age of 33 years of age. He did not live much longer to enjoy the fruits of his gallant victories. He was plagued with health challenges including malaria and typhoid fever. At a celebration in Babylon which he now ruled, in the palace of Nebuchadnezzar II, Alexander worked himself into a drunken stupor. He never recovered from his drunkenness. It resulted in his death. Alexander had no heirs to assume the headship of his kingdom as was customary of the times in which he lived. There was none to carry on his legacy as he had done after the death of his father, Phillip of Macedonia. In his dying moments, his generals asked him, "To whom do you leave the kingdom?" He replied, "To the best, to the strongest." That was exactly what happened.

Following Alexander's death, much infighting among his top generals erupted. His four strongest generals, Ptolemy Lagus, Seleucus, Nicator, Cassander, and Lysimachus divided his empire among themselves. The leopard with four wings and four heads as portrayed in Daniel's dream (Daniel 7:6) aptly describes the swiftness and skill with which Alexander the Great conquered the world. It is also a fitting description of the subsequent dividing-up of the empire among Alexander's four strongest generals. Daniel's prophecy concerning the third beast (kingdom) is thus perfectly fulfilled.

As Daniel proceeds with the account of his vision, he describes the fourth beast. He tells us, "After this, I saw in the night vision, and behold a fourth beast dreadful and terrible, and strong exceedingly and it had great iron teeth: it devoured and brake in pieces, and stamped the residue with the feet of it: and it was diverse from all the beasts that was before it: and it had ten horns" (Daniel 7:7). Some three years later God again gave Daniel a vision which confirmed what he dreamt previously. It gave more detail of the fourth beast which was to rule the world until the second coming of Jesus Christ. I quote from the inspired record, "In the third year of the reign of King Belshazzar, a vision appeared unto me, even unto me Daniel, after that which appeared unto me first" (Daniel 8:1). It is here clearly indicated that Daniel's second dream was in connection with the first. This time however, only two beasts are portrayed. The prophet records, "Then I lifted up mine eyes and saw, and behold a ram which had two horns: and the horns were high: but one was higher than the other, and the higher came up last… I saw the ram pushing westward, and northward, and southward; so that no beast might stand before him, neither was there any that could deliver out of his hand, but he did according to his will, and became great" (Daniel 8:3).

Then Daniel saw another beast (nation) coming against the first kingdom, the ram. He relates, "And as I was considering, behold an he goat came from the west on the face of the whole earth, and touched not the ground: And the goat had a notable horn between his eyes… And he came to the ram that had the two horns, which I had seen standing before the river, and ran unto him in the fury of his power... And I saw him come close unto the ram, and he was moved with choler against him, and smote the ram, and brake his two horns: and there was no power in the ram to stand before, but he cast him down to the ground, and stamped upon him; and there was none that could deliver the ram out of his hand... therefore the he goat waxed very great. And when he was strong the great horn was broken: and for it came up four notable ones towards the four winds of heaven" (Daniel 8:5-8). Daniel is here referring to the military conflicts between Media/Persia resulting in Alexander the Great conquering the Media/Persian Empire. He in fact goes on to identify those two beasts (nations) by name: Media/ Persia (Daniel 8:20) and Greece (Daniel 8:21).

Next, Daniel saw a little horn (young nation) emerging out of one of the four divisions of the Grecian Empire. It ultimately grew stronger and more powerful than both the ram and the goat. Of this kingdom, Daniel writes, "and out of one of them came forth a little horn, which waxed exceeding great, toward the south, and toward the east and toward the pleasant land...and it waxed great even to the host of heaven: and it cast down some of the host and of the stars to the ground and stamped upon them. Yea, he magnified himself even to the prince of the host, and by him the daily sacrifice was taken away, and the place of the sanctuary was cast down. And an host was given him against the daily sacrifice by reason of transgression, and it cast down the truth to the ground; and it practiced, and prospered" (Daniel 8:9-12).

As Daniel foresaw the work of this little horn (nation) but did not quite understand its significance, the angel Gabriel was sent to give him the full interpretation of his dream. Daniel relates, "And I heard a man's voice between the banks of the Ulai which called, and said, Gabriel, make this man to understand the vision...And he said, Behold I will make thee to know what shall be in the last end of the indignation for at the time appointed the end shall be...The Ram which thou sawest having the two horns are the kings of Media and Persia... And the rough goat is the king of Grecia: and the great horn that is between his eyes is the first king...Now that being broken, whereas four stood up for it, four kingdoms shall stand up out of the Nation, but not in his power" (Daniel 8:21,22).

Gabriel reveals to Daniel more detail about the fourth kingdom, "And in the latter time of their kingdom when transgressions are come to the full, a king of fierce countenance, and understanding dark sentences shall stand up and his power shall be mighty but not of his own power: and he shall destroy wonderful, and shall prosper and practice and shall destroy the mighty and the holy people" (Daniel 8:23,24).

Daniel's dreams, the second confirming and expanding upon the first, foretold the kingdoms that would rule the world and have significant impact upon God's people and His plan of human redemption. We have clearly identified the first three beasts (kingdoms) of Daniel 7 to be (1) Babylon (2) Media/Persia and (3) Greece. We have also identified the two beasts (kingdoms) of Daniel 8 to also be Media/Persia and Greece. These nations, beginning with Babylon, successively conquered each other to become the ruling world power of their time. Each conquered more territory and dominated more people than the one preceding it. Babylon ruled from 606 B.C. to 536 B.C. It was followed by Media/Persia, which ruled from 536 B.C. to 331 B.C. Media/Persia was conquered by Alexander the Great. The Grecian empire extended from 331 B.C. to about 168 B.C. These are documented historical facts.

But who is the nation that followed them? What nation is the fourth beast of Daniel 7 and the king of fierce countenance, and the little horn of Daniel chapter 8? Since the dream of Daniel 7 is consistent with the vision of Daniel 8, then the nations portrayed by these symbols must also be identical. The Biblical and historical records with regards to Babylon, Media/Persia, and Greece have been undeniably established.

The popular Roman Catholic teaching, adopted with the vast majority Christian teachers, is that the 'Little Horn' is Antiochus Epiphanes. However, reason, common sense, and the historical record firmly dictate otherwise.

The prophecy foretells that Media/Persia would be great. Then it states that Greece would be very great. The Little Horn, which arises after Greece, Daniel states, would become exceedingly great. Here are four historical facts that demolish the idea that Antiochus Epiphanes is the Little Horn of Daniel's prophecy:

1. For the Little Horn to become exceedingly great it would have to conquer more territory and rule over more people than Media/ Persia (Great) and Greece (Very Great). Antiochus Epiphanes was one of about twenty five petty kings who grew out of the Seleucid Dynasty, one of the four divisions of Alexander the Great divided empire. That area is known today as Syria.

2. The prophecy states that the Little Horn power would stand up against the Prince of Princes (Daniel 8:25). The Prince of Princes is Jesus Christ. (Revelation 1:5; 17:14; 19:16). Antiochus Epiphanes died around the year 164 B.C., well before the first advent of Jesus Christ.

3. Daniel also states that it would also cast down the sanctuary and the truth to the ground (Daniel 8:11-12). Those that point to Antiochus Epiphanes as the Little Horn conclude that Antiochus' desecrating the Jewish temple in Jerusalem fulfills this prophecy. Since the Little Horn Power stands up against Jesus Christ, the Prince of Princes and Prince of Hosts, that assertion must be false. For the sanctuary here being referred to could not be the ancient Israeli sanctuary; but rather the heavenly sanctuary where Jesus sits as our High Priest (Hebrews 4:14-17). The truth being cast down is that Jesus Christ is our Only High Priest and Mediator between us and God (1Timothy 1:5).

4. If Antiochus was the Little Horn power that became exceedingly great after the world empire of Alexander the Great, why would he be forced to pay taxes to the Romans as stated in the Encyclopedia of Religious Knowledge? "Finding his resources exhausted, he [Antiochus] resolved to into Persia, to levy tributes and collect large sums which he had agreed to pay to the Romans".

That Little Horn Power, which grew out of Alexander the Great divided empire, and to which Antiochus Epiphanes was forced to pay taxes must be some entity much greater and powerful than not only Antiochus Epiphanes; but verily the kingdom of Alexander the Great, from which it sprung. There is only one entity that fits that description in every particular, and that is indeed the Imperial Roman Empire.

CHAPTER 5

The Abomination of Desolation

ollowing the world rule of Greece, and the dividing-up of Alexander the Great Empire by his four most powerful generals, history records the rapid rise of a small, seemingly insignificant tribe coming out from banks of the River Tiber. It rose with swiftness and might to become the world's dominating power in less than 200 years. Legends abound about the birth and formative years of this power. What is not in doubt, nor is at all legend, is its rise to world greatness and dominance. According to God's Word, that kingdom will rise, its character will be transformed, and then rule the world once again in the last days of earth's history. Her resurgence to world dominance will last until the second coming of Our Lord and Savior, Jesus Christ. As it rises to universal power, that kingdom will enforce its mark of authority upon all men on planet earth. All will submit to her authority, except those, who by faith, receive the seal of authority of the God of creation and have their names written in His book of life. (Revelation 13:8).

The prophet Daniel, in Daniel 7:7, (quoted earlier) describes a nation that was unlike anything he had seen previously in his vision. It was a mighty nation with immense military power. It conquered all the other kingdoms that were before it to ascend to the ruler ship of the world. It moved with swiftness, cruelty and determined fierceness to crush its opponents and control its conquered prey. Likewise, in his vision of Daniel 8, the prophet refers to the same kingdom thus, "and out of one of them (the four divisions of Alexander the Great Greek Empire/the He goat) came forth a little horn, which waxed exceeding great, toward the south and toward the east, and toward the pleasant land" (Daniel 8:9). Historical evidence supports the fact that the Roman empire was the dominating power that arose after the Grecian empire. Rome extended its power to the south (Egypt), to the east (Macedonia), and to the 'pleasant land' (Palestine). No other power matches this description.

The characteristics of the fourth beast are synonymous, in every particular, with one entity and one entity only. That is the Roman Empire, first in its Pagan form and then its Papal form. It is the only nation that rose from obscurity to rule the world with a mighty fist for more than 600 years. Rome indeed grew exceedingly great and stood up to the "Prince of the host, Jesus Christ." It was the Roman Empire, in its pagan form that crucified our Savior and destroyed the Jewish temple. In its Papal form, it caused the heavenly sanctuary to be 'cast down' by instituting a system of earthly priests in the place of our Heavenly High Priest, Jesus Christ. History testifies that the Roman Empire arose on the heels of the Grecian empire to rule the world with an iron fist. Imperial Rome is, without a doubt, the kingdom that followed the world reign of Greece.

The history of the Roman people can be traced back to more than 1000 years B.C. But, it was their bloody victories in the Punic wars, culminating in their conquest of Spain, North Africa, Greece, Asia Minor and Egypt that established Rome as a world empire around the year 149 BC. This is the nation that is brought to view in Daniel's dream of Daniel 7:7, and his vision of Daniel 8:9, quoted earlier. The conquests of Imperial Rome were magnanimous. They are thus aptly described by the prophet. Any challenge to her supremacy was swiftly subdued. All opposition to her authority was eradicated. The strong arm of her legendary military might was uncontestable.

Daniel continues his portrayal of this power: "I considered the horns, and behold, there came up among them another little horn, before whom there were three of the first horns plucked up by the roots; and, behold, in this horn were eyes like the eyes of man, and a mouth speaking great things" (Daniel 7:8). He reiterates this series of events in his vision of Daniel 8. He relates, "And it waxed great, even to the host of heaven; and it cast down some of the host and of the stars to the ground, and stamped upon them. Yea, he magnified himself even to the Prince of the host, and by him the daily was taken away and the place of his sanctuary was cast down...And in the latter time of their kingdom, when the transgressions are come to the full, a king of fierce countenance, and understanding dark sentences, shall stand up. And his power shall be mighty but not by his own power: and he shall destroy wonderfully, and shall prosper and practice, and shall destroy the mighty and holy people" (Daniel 8: 10, 11-12 & 23-24).

In both of these accounts, Daniel is portraying a change in the nature of this kingdom. It is a change from its militaristic nature to one of a religious nature. This is especially true and accurate of the Roman Empire. Rome's transformation from a world military power into the world's most dominant religion of its time is undeniable. Historian Will Durant writes, " When Christianity conquered Rome, the ecclesiastical structure of the pagan church, the title and vestments of the Pontifex Maximus, the worship of the Great Mother goddess and a multitude of comforting divinities… the joy and solemnity of old festivals, and the pageantry of immemorial ceremony, passed like maternal blood into the new religion, and captive Rome captured her conqueror. The reigns and skills of government were handed down by a dying empire to a virile Papacy. The lost power of the broken sword was re-won by the magic of the consoling word. The armies of the state were replaced by the missionaries of the church, moving in all directions along the Roman roads; and the revolted provinces, accepting Christianity, again acknowledged the sovereignty of Rome. The church with the shadow of the ancient authority behind it was the only symbol left of imperial Rome. Its bishop, the pope of Rome, was the city's only recourse for leadership and protection. The Roman Empire in Europe would be replaced by the spiritual empire, which came to be temporal as well, whose reigning seigneur was the bishop of Rome" (Caesar and Christ, page 672).

Unlike the previous world kingdoms (Babylon, Media/Persia, and Greece), the Roman Empire was not conquered by another world power. It changed structure from pagan to papal. This is what Daniel sees as he reports on the fourth beast having ten horns. (Daniel 7: 7,8) The pagan Roman Empire reached its zenith in about the fourth century AD. At about this time, it began to lose its military and political grip on the nations that comprised the empire. The empire's decline was troubled and slow, bottoming out about 476 AD. As the pagan empire declined, the church grew more and more powerful, eventually taking control of the empire in its papal or religious form. Historian Alexander C. Flick records, "The mighty Catholic Church was little more than the Roman Empire baptized. Rome was transformed as well as converted. It is not a matter of great surprise, therefore, to find that from the first to the fourth century, the church had undergone many changes" (Rise of the Medieval Church, page 148,149).

The empire's resources and attention were now directed towards resisting the marauding barbarian tribes in her midst. These tribes grew more and more independent of the political seat of power in Rome. Eventually, they carved up the empire unto ten divisions, loosely connected to the imperial monarchy. The empire was eventually divided into the eastern half and the western half.

The western empire, today known as Western Europe, was for all intents and purposes, under the control of the church which inherited its authority from the waning pagan military structure. Such developments allowed for the further political independence of those tribes comprising the Western Empire. What kept them together was the burgeoning influence and authority of the church. What military might and political strategy failed to accomplish, the religion of the church achieved. Below are those tribes with their corresponding modern names:

Visigoths—Spain
Lombards—Italy
Anglo Saxons—England
Franks—France
Alemani—Germany
Burgundians—Switzerland
Suevi—Portugal
Heruli—Uprooted. No modern counterpart
Ostrogoths—Uprooted. No modern counterpart
Vandals—Uprooted. No modern counterpart

Even as the military might of Rome was waning and its political strength disintegrating, the increasingly powerful church provided the glue that held the nations together. That glue was religion. From the time of Constantine's supposed acceptance of Christianity, in the early 4th century, the pure religion of Christ was amalgamated with prevailing, customary pagan religious practices. This mix of

Christianity and paganism was advanced by the use of what military strength was retained by the individual tribes. Foremost in support of the church and its religion was the Franks and their king, Clovis. Of the ten emerging nations of the former unified empire, three – Heruli, Vandals and Ostroghoths, opposed the teachings and authority of the burgeoning church. They followed the leadings of Arius, a bishop of Alexandria, Egypt who refused to accept, among other things, the church's teaching of the Trinity and the Divinity of Jesus Christ.

For these reasons, those three nations were rooted up by the church, utilizing the military force of those who agreed with her and were under her control. Such is represented by Daniel's account of the little horn that uprooted three of the ten horns (Daniel 7:8). That little horn is representative of the emerging church. It not only filled the vacuum left by the declining pagan empire; but it grew to become even more powerful and vicious. The last one of those nations/horns, the Ostrogoths, was obliterated and vanished from Rome and the history books in 538 AD. The church would later annihilate more than 50 million people, according to some accounts, who would not follow its teachings that salvation can only be obtained through her and not Jesus Christ alone as the Bible teaches.

The Emperor Justinian, having had the laws of the empire rewritten (Justinian Decree, AD 533) to accommodate the growing power of the church, finally ceded full and complete control to her in that very year. This marked the transfer from Imperial Rome to Papal Rome, today called the Papacy. What the Caesars could not achieve through military might and political scheming, the Papacy accomplished though the force of apostate religion—-reunification of the nations of Western Europe.

Daniel details the workings and development of the little horn (the Papacy). "And of the ten horns that were in his head, and of the other which came up, and before whom three fell: even of that horn that had eyes, and a mouth that spoke very great things, whose look was more stout than his fellows... I beheld and the same horn made war with the saints and prevailed against them, until the Ancient of days come and judgment was given to the saints of the Most High and the time came that the saints possessed the kingdom. ...And he (the little horn/the Papacy) shall speak great words against the most High, and shall wear out the saints of the most High and think to change times and laws; and they shall be given into his hand until a time and times the dividing of time" (Daniel 7: 20, 21, 22, 25).

Here is a summary of Daniel's description and the historical record of the little horn, the Papacy that emerged from the divided fourth kingdom, the Roman Empire.

> It would up-root three of the ten horns/nations of divided Rome (Daniel 7:8).
> It would have at its head, a man who speaks for it and has full authority over it (Daniel 7:8, 20).
> It would be diverse (different) from the other ten horns. (Daniel 7:24)
> It would persecute God's people (Daniel 7:25).
> It would speak great words (blaspheme) against God (Daniel 7:25).
> It would attempt to change God's law (Daniel 7:25).

These points of identification relate to one power, and one power alone—Roman Church/State. It is today known as Papacy. This is the 'BEAST." It is, as the Protestant Reformers maintained, the antichrist power of Bible prophecy. This is perhaps shocking, but true. Both the historical record and Biblical prophecy confirm this fact. It must be carefully noted here that the above characterization does not apply to the tens of millions of godly people who sincerely believe they are serving God by being part of this organization. We are referring to a system and hierarchy whose existence conforms to the historical facts and Biblical prophecy.

Daniel's prophecy perfectly complements the characterization given by John the Revelator: " So he carried me away in the wilderness: and I saw a woman sit upon a scarlet colored beast, full of names of blasphemy, having seven heads and ten horns" (Revelation 17:3). John, like Daniel, refers to the element of blasphemy connected to this power. Blasphemy is a religious term. It implies speaking against the God of creation or purporting to take the prerogatives of His office. For example, we find that Jesus, having healed a man from his paralytic condition, proceeded to forgive his sins. Luke reports, "And when He saw their faith, He said unto him, 'man, thy sins are forgiven thee'. And the Scribes and the Pharisees began to reason, 'saying who is this, which speaks blasphemies? Who can forgive sins, but God alone?" (Luke 5:21). Of course, Jesus was not speaking blasphemy. He was verily God in the flesh. Therefore, the privilege to forgive men of their sins is exclusively His. The idea of claiming to forgive other men of their sins is the prerogative of God and God only. Jesus also declares, "Me and my Father are one" (John 10:30). The Jews reacted to Jesus' assertion by taking up stones to stone him to death. What was their reason? John reports, "The Jews answered him saying, 'for a good work we stone thee not: but for blasphemy; and because that thou, being a man makes thyself God" (John 10:30).

But the church on the seven hills teaches, "The Pope is not only the representative of Jesus Christ, but he is Jesus Christ Himself, hidden under the veil of flesh" (The Catholic Standard, July 1895). She continues, "When the pope is crowned, he is reminded that he is the father of princess, and kings, and the supreme ruler of the universe, and on the earth, the vicar of Jesus Christ our Savior, and the Governor of the world"(Ecclesiastical Dictionary, Lucius Ferraris, 1763). Notice also this declaration regarding the Roman Catholic priesthood, "The Priest holds the place of the Savior himself, when, by saying "ego te absolvo" (I thee absolve), he absolves from sin...to pardon a single sin requires all the omnipotence of God... But what only God can do by His omnipotence, the priest can do by saying 'ego te absolvo a peccatis tuis'" (Dignities and Duties of the Priest, pages 34, 36). Further, the woman on the seven mountains claims, "Thus the priest, in a certain manner, is called the creator of his creator. The power of the priest is the power of the divine person; for the transubstantiation of the bread requires as much power as the creation of the world" (ibid., pages 32, 33).

One can hardly get any more blasphemous than that. Such is the nature of the beast. These are the pronouncements of the Church of Rome. John continues, "And the beast which I saw was like unto a leopard, and his feet were the feet of a bear, and the mouth as the mouth of a lion: and the dragon gave him his power, and his seat, and great authority" (Revelation 13:2). Here, John is describing the Papacy as having the religious characteristics and embodying the practices of the world's ruling powers that immediately preceded her.

Looking back down the prophetic timeline, John sees the Roman power, in its papal form, as possessing and practicing the policies, beliefs, and dogmas of Greece (the leopard), Media/Persia (the bear) and Babylon (the lion). These were the nations that ruled, in reverse order, before the Roman Empire (Daniel 7:4-7). Daniel also confirms this fact. He declares, "As concerning the rest of the beasts they had their dominion taken away: yet their lives were prolonged for a season and time" (Daniel 7:12). In other words, both Daniel and John are saying that the religious and political elements of Babylon, Media/Persia and Greece were adopted into the Roman Empire, and ultimately amalgamated into the Papacy. Most strikingly, however, John not only declares that all the abominations of the previous world empires reside in the Papacy; but he also states that she gets her power and authority from the dragon. And who is the dragon? Inspiration answers, "And the great dragon was cast out, that old serpent, called the devil, and Satan (Revelation 12:9).

The Papacy, the Bible explains, gets its power and authority from the devil himself. Like Satan, all its schemes are but a masterpiece of deception designed to usurp the authority of God in men's hearts. It seeks to receive the worship of men that only God deserves. In further describing that entity, John relates, "And I saw one of his heads as it were wounded to death; and his deadly wound was healed; and all the world wondered after the beast...And they worshiped the dragon which gave power unto the beast; and they worshiped the beast saying, who is like unto the beast? Who is able to make war with him" (Revelation 13:3,4). The wound is, at least in part, an obvious reference to the great Protestant Reformation. This Bible-based, Holy-Spirit led, opposition movement posed a formidable challenge to the universal reign of the Papacy with her pagan traditions and spurious religious doctrines. More precisely, however, the deadly wound refers to the dismantling of the Papacy under Napoleon Bonaparte.

The year was 1798. Napoleon, utterly disgusted with the domination of the church and determined to conquer the world, sent his most-able general, Louis Berthier, into the city of Rome. The then ruling Pope, Pope Pius VI was taken prisoner by Berthier and exiled to Valence, France where he (Pope Pius VI) died in 1799. In effect, what Napoleon accomplished was the taking away of the political/military power from the Papacy. He declared it to be a religious entity only. By this act, Napoleon neutralized the power of the church over the states. That act constituted the deadly wound——the separation of the political/military from the ecclesiastical. Slowly, but stealthily, the Papacy set out to regain its lost position as ruler of the nations. The healing of the wound was manifested in earnest in February 1929.

In that year, the Roman Church signed an agreement with Premier Benito Mussolini of Italy. He was one of her most faithful and dedicated sons. The agreement is called the Lateran Treaty.

That action effectively restored the political power of the Papacy by declaring it a nation unto itself. Of course, it always retained its seemingly religious character. The Associated Press headlined the occasion, "Mussolini and Gasparri sign historic Roman Pact...heal wound of many years." The story, appearing on February 11, 1929 stated, "The Roman question tonight was a thing of the past and the Vatican was at peace with Italy. The formal accomplishment of this today, was the exchange of signatures in the historic palace of St. John Lateran by two noteworthy plenipotentiaries, Cardinal Gasparri for Pope Pius XI and Premier Mussolini for King Emmanuel III." The San Francisco Chronicle reported on February 12, 1929, "In affixing the autographs to the memorable document, healing the wound which has festered since 1870, extreme cordiality, was displayed on both sides."

It is breathtakingly remarkable that secular news sources, with no reference to Biblical prophecy, used the very words of Scripture in describing the reemergence of the Papacy as a world political entity. Who can doubt that since that time, the Roman Church has grown rapidly into a dominant world political player? Her religious influence has permeated every corner of the world. Presidents and kings, princes and prime ministers, men and women everywhere bow down in blind obedience and reverence to the Pope of Rome. The late Pope John Paul II epitomized this phenomenon best as he traveled from country to country, promoting the persona of the most trusted, and pious religious leader in the world. Pope Francis continues on the same path. Who can forget that well publicized scene of three American presidents kneeling at the coffin, paying homage, to a dead John Paul II? How sad is it that Christians everywhere, while claiming Jesus as their Savior, are bowing down and worshiping the Pope of Rome as their Lord.

As pointed out earlier, recognizing Sunday sacredness is the ultimate sign of servitude to the Pope of Rome. The apostle Paul reminds us, "Know ye not, that to whom ye yield yourselves servants to obey, his servants ye are to whom ye obey; whether of sin unto death, or of obedience unto righteousness?" (Romans 16:16). We worship God by keeping His commandments. Jesus declares, "If ye love me, keep my commandments" (John 14:15). The wise man Solomon agrees, "Let us hear the conclusion of the whole matter: Fear God, and keep His commandments; for this is the whole duty of man" (Ecclesiastes 12:13).

God has given us His Ten Commandments. He requires us to keep them all. This includes keeping holy His Sabbath-day, the 7th day of the week. God calls His Sabbath-day a sign between Him and His people (Exodus 31:17). It is the seal of His law in which He places His name, His title and His territory of dominion. (Exodus 20: 8-11) Roman Catholicism, the antichrist power of Bible prophecy, says not so. She declares, exactly as Daniel prophesied in Daniel 7:25, that she would attempt to change God's law. She further declares that that change is her mark of authority. In the Converts Catholicism, the Roman Catholic premier teaching source for her followers, we find the following:

Question: Which is the Sabbath day?
Answer: Saturday is the Sabbath-day.
Question: Why do we observe Sunday instead of Saturday?
Answer: We observe Sunday instead of Saturday because the Catholic Church transferred the solemnity from Saturday to Sunday.

The God of creation neither authorizes nor give any human instrument the authority to change His law. Such blasphemous declarations are in direct opposition to God's Word and are therefore manifestations of the spirit of antichrist who seeks to take the place of Christ. Men may try, but it is impossible to change God's law.

The audacity of this power has led the Papacy to make this boastful claim. She affirms, "Of course, the Catholic Church claims that the change was her act. And the act is a "MARK" of her ecclesiastical power and authority in religious matters." (Letter from Cardinal James Gibbons of Baltimore). She continues: "Sunday is our MARK of authority. The church is above the Bible, and this transference of Sabbath observance is proof of that fact" (The Catholic Record, September 1, 1929) Furthermore, the late Pope John Paul II declared in His apostolic letter of July 1998, "The celebration of the Christian Sunday remains on the threshold of the third millennium, an indispensable element of our Christian identity" (Dies Domini, Section 30).

God says that the Sabbath is the sign of His authority. His inspired Word reveals no concept of a Christian Sunday. That is the mark of apostasy. The Pope says Sunday is the mark of his authority. The question is: whom are you following? The late Pope John Paul II further issued a not so veiled threat to those who do not go along with his church's Sunday command, "Christians will naturally strive to ensure that civil legislation respects their duty to keep Sabbath (Sunday) holy" (ibid., Section 67).

The plain fact is that only God can make a day holy. The day He has made holy is the seventh day, today called Saturday. It is the only, holy Sabbath-day. Make no mistake, this legislation attempting to establish Sunday in place of God's Sabbath will be implemented around the world. God's Word prophesies it. Its violation will be punishable by imprisonment and death. The church has declared that anyone not abiding by her Sunday decree will be treated as a heretic. You need only to take a look at her past history to see how heretics were treated. They were burned alive at the stake, quartered at the rack, boiled in oil, fed to hungry, wild animals, fed to rats, beheaded at the guillotine and subjected to other devilish devices too numerous to mention. Such actions characterize the church's actions of old. She has not changed the dogmas that led to such atrocities. She will not hesitate to do them again when vantage ground is granted to her.

Contrary to her public persona, the Church of Rome has not changed. She covers the iron hand of intolerance and persecution with the velvet glove of religion. Her spirit of religious intolerance and insatiable lust for world domination are the underpinnings of her aims and purposes. Says one historian, "That the Church of Rome has shed more innocent blood than any other institution that have ever existed among mankind, will be questioned by no Protestant who has a competent knowledge of history...It is impossible to form a complete conception of the multitude of her victims, and it is quite certain that no powers of imagination can adequately realize their sufferings" (History of The Rise and Influence of The Spirit of Rationalism in Europe, W.E.H. Lecky, Volume 2, page 32, 1910 ed).

Pope John Paul's declaration in Dies Domini is no empty threat. When the Papacy will have once again orchestrated its rise to the governorship of the world, then all will know the true nature of the beast. Then all will have to choose. Your choice will have to be between the God of creation and His holy Sabbath-day (His seal), and the Pope of Rome, who claims to be God with his Sunday sacredness. (Its mark of authority). The final, and perhaps most revealing trait of the beast, is John's characterization of its leader. He declares, "Here is wisdom. Let him that hath understanding count the number of the beast: for it is the number of a man; and his number is six hundred three score and six" (Revelation 13:18). That is 666.

When someone is elected Pope, he is crowned with a triple crown signifying his lordship of the heavens above, the earth we live on, and the regions below. He assumes the title – VICARIUS FILII DEI, Vicar of the Son of God. The numerical equivalent of that Roman title is as follows:

V-5, I-1, C-100, A-0, R-0, I-1, U-5, S-0 =	112
F-0, I-1, L-50, I-1, I-1 =	53
D-500, E-0, I-1 =	501
Total	666

How remarkable. The Pope is referred to as the Vicar of Christ. This title is translated to mean He who takes the place of God on earth. And who is it that Isaiah says seeks to take the place of God? (Isaiah 14:12-17) The prophet declares that it is the devil, the ultimate antichrist. The identification of 'the beast' and its mark is complete, accurate and undeniable.

But, the Protestant Reformers recognized this power to be exactly what the Bible declares it to be, the anti-Christ power of Bible prophecy. Martin Luther declared, "We here are of the conviction that the Papacy is the seat of the true and real anti- Christ...personally, I declare that I owe the pope no other obedience than that to anti-Christ" (Prophetic Faith of our Fathers, LeRoy Edwin Froom, Vol. 2.pg 121). John Wesley agrees, "He (the pope) is in an emphatic sense, the Man of Sin, as he increases all manner of sin above measure. And so he is, too, properly styled the Son of Perdition as he has caused the death of numberless multitudes, both of his opposers and followers. He it is that exalteth himself above all that is called Christ, or that is worshipped...claiming the highest power and highest honor... claiming the prerogatives which belong to God alone" (Antichrist and his Ten Kingdoms, John Wesley, pg 110). John Calvin joins the chorus, "Some persons think us too severe and censorious when we call the Roman pontiff anti-Christ. But those who are of this opinion do not consider that they bring the same charge of presumption against Paul himself, after whom we speak and whose language we adopt... I shall briefly show that Paul's words in 2 Thessalonians 2 are not capable of any other interpretation than that which applies to the Papacy" (Institutes, John Calvin).

The sentiments expressed by Luther, Wesley, and Calvin were identical to those of John Knox of Scotland, Thomas Cramer of England, Roger Williams of the United States and the entire Protestant Reformation movement. It is too sad that Christians today have not only lost sight of the Reformation; but are seeking the aid of the Papacy in their zeal to have the government institute religious laws. Exactly as was prophesied, we have shown from the historical record, the power that claims the prerogative to change God's holy Sabbath day from the seventh day of the week to the first.

One of the most overlooked prophetic events that Jesus Christ shared with His disciples (and with us today), when asked what would be the signs of His coming and of the end of the world, is the Abomination of Desolation spoken of by the prophet Daniel (Matthew 24:15). The Abomination of Desolation may be a mystery to many and certainly there is much speculation surrounding it. But Jesus was simply referring to a system of salvation that would be set up which is contrary to and in opposition to His ONLY way of salvation, i.e. by God's grace through faith in His Son and our Savior, Jesus Christ (John 14:6; Acts 4:12). That prophecy is being fulfilled right before our very eyes; and most of the world, including the majority of Christendom, is totally oblivious to this phenomenon of apocalyptic proportions.

Not only does Daniel clearly identify the power that would seek to establish such a system (Daniel 8:9-13); but the apostle Paul gives us further clarification, "Let no man deceive you by any means: for that day shall not come, except there come a falling away first, and that man of sin be revealed, the son of perdition; Who opposeth and exalteth himself above all that is called God, or that is worshipped; so that he as God sitteth in the temple of God, shewing himself that he is God. (2 Thessalonians 2:3-4). The evidence thus far presented identifies that entity to be none other than the Roman Papacy.

Here is the undeniable proof. Pope Francis, in addressing a gathering of more than 33,000 at the Vatican on Wednesday, 25 June 2014, declared: "...There are those who believe they can maintain a personal, direct and immediate relationship with Jesus Christ outside the communion and the mediation of the Church. These are dangerous and harmful temptations... Dear friends, let us ask the Lord, through the intercession of the Virgin Mary, Mother of the Church, for the grace never to fall into the temptation of thinking we can make it without the others, that we can get along without the Church, that we can save ourselves on our own, of being Christians from the laboratory..."

This declaration of the Pope should awaken the sleeping saints to his and his church's real objective. It was this very policy that led to its slaughter to tens of millions of innocent Christians who disagreed with her and rejected her false system of salvation during the Dark Ages.

The Bible's description of an abomination is that of someone, fully knowing the truth of what God's says, blatantly chooses to do otherwise. That abomination always leads to desolation or destruction. That being the case, the Papacy's abomination of seeking to establish Sunday sacredness in place of God's Sabbath truth and denying Jesus as the only way of salvation will not lead to peace, unity, and tranquility as she promises; but will result in tyranny, confusion, and destruction such as the world has never seen. That is the final Abomination of Desolation that Jesus warned about. (Matthew 24:15). Please take heed.

CHAPTER 6

The United States in Bible Prophecy

Now that the beast (The Roman Papacy) and its mark (Sunday sacredness) have been identified; let's take a look at America and the prophetic role this nation is fulfilling in the world today. The apostle John, in the thirteenth chapter of the Book of Revelation, gives us clearer evidence of the time of rule of Roman Catholicism. As we discussed in the previous chapter, that in the year 1798, its reign came to a halt. That was at the hands of Napoleon's general, Louis Berthier. He marched into Rome, arrested Pope Pius VI, and exiled him to Valence, France where he eventually died. This constituted the deadly wound (Revelation 13:3). The healing of the wound, or certainly the beginning thereof, was shown to be the agreement made between Premier Mussolini of Italy and the Papacy in the year 1929. John the Revelator re-emphasizes the point of the wounding of the beast. He states, "He that leadeth into captivity, shall go into captivity: he that killeth with the sword, must be killed with the sword: Here is the patience and the faith of the Saints" (Revelation 13: 10). Just about the time that the beast from the sea (Roman Catholicism arising out of the populated areas of Western Europe, Revelation 13:1) is wounded (loses its political ability), John reports that another beast (nation) arises from the earth. But what nation does this earth-beast represent? John continues, "And I beheld another beast, coming out of the earth and he had two horns like a lamb and he spoke as a dragon" (Revelation 13: 11).

The sea, as the Bible points out, represents people, nations and tongues (Revelation 17:15). This is a reference to a well-populated area of the world. All the nations, that we have discussed thus far, arose from populated areas and ascended to the world stage through strife and conquest. But this nation comes out of the earth. This is in contrast to the nations that came out of the sea.

The only justifiable conclusion that can be drawn about this nation is that it arose out of an unpopulated area of the world. Of all the other nations mentioned by Daniel and John, none is referred to as having as part of their character, a notion of worshipping the true God. This nation, coming out of the earth, however, is described as having two horns like a lamb. A lamb in Scripture refers to Jesus. The apostle John, referring to Jesus, at the time of His baptism, records, "The next day John saw Jesus coming unto him, and said 'Behold the Lamb of God, which takes away the sin of the world" (John 1:29).

The idea of Revelation 13:11, as presented by John, is that of a nation professing Christian qualities and arising out of an unpopulated area. John also places the birth of this nation in the time frame of the demise of the Papacy. There is one nation and one nation only that fits these specifications. That nation is undoubtedly the United States of America.

John Wesley, earlier in the same century, writes of the nation that was to arise after the Papacy, "He has not yet come, though he cannot be afar off. For he is to appear at the end of the forty-two months of the first beast" (Explanatory Notes on the New Testament, John Wesley, page 735). The forty-two months is in reality 1260 years, extending from 538 AD to 1798 AD. It has already been established that this period was the time period of Roman Catholicism's dark reign over the world. Forty- two prophetic months (1260 days) is equivalent to 1260 literal years (30 days per month x 42 months) The prophet Moses explains, "After the number of the days in which ye searched the land, even forty days, each day for a year, shall ye bear your iniquities, even forty years, and ye shall know my breach of promise" (Numbers 14:34) (See also Ezekiel 4:6). Utilizing this prophetic yardstick, we clearly see the prophetic accuracy of the reign of the Papacy. It was officially established in 538 AD when Emperor Justinian decreed the Catholic Church to have complete control over the empire. Its rule extended to 1798 AD, when Napoleon's general, Berthier, deposed Pope Pius VI. This period is precisely 1260 years.

John the Revelator also confirms this time period. In referring to the period of Papal persecution of God's people, he writes, "And the woman (God's true church) fled into the wilderness, where she hath a place prepared of God, that they should feed her for a thousand, two hundred and three score days" (Revelation 12:6). This is exactly as the Scriptures foretold it to be, 1260 years.

When we consider the events that gave birth to the United States of America, the accuracy of this prophecy is undeniably accurate and fascinating. The struggle of the American Colonies for independence began in 1775. In 1776 the Declaration of Independence was signed and the founding fathers declared the United States of America to be an independent nation. In 1777 the Articles of Confederation were adopted. In 1787 the U.S. Constitution was framed. On July 26, 1788 it was ratified by the original 13 states. On the first of March 1789, the U.S. Constitution went into effect. This was all taking place as the Papacy was losing its hold on the people of the world as a result of the Protestant Reformation.

The United States was emerging not only as a new nation, but also as a bastion of freedom for those who were fleeing the pangs of popery in the Old World. People fled Europe by the thousands. They sought to find a nation without a Pope and a country without a king. They risked their very lives to move to a country in which they would not have to be enslaved by the dogmas of the Pope and his church, or be controlled by the tyranny of kings and princes who persecuted them on behalf of the Pope. Civil War author and journalist, George Alfred Townsend, writes, "the history of the United States was separated by a beneficent providence far from this wild and cruel history of the rest of the continent" (The New World Compared With The New, page 633). In a similar tone, journalist Charles Summer wrote the following words in an article in the Atlantic Monthly of September 1886. He described the emergence of the United States of America thus, "A revolution that has stranger marks of divine interposition, superseding the ordinary course of human affairs, than any other event which the world had experienced."

America's birth was indeed somewhat different from the world powers that preceded it. Yes, there were the revolutionary conflicts and the exploitation and massacre of the Native Americans. But those can hardly be compared to the strife that characterized the emergence of previous world powers of Babylon, Media/ Persia, Greece, and Rome. America was born as a nation that provided a sanctuary for those fleeing political and religious persecution from the kings and popes of Europe. Such was the rise of America. In addition to its youthfulness and seeming Christian character, John declares that this nation would one day speak like a dragon. He also portrays this emerging nation as having two horns like a lamb. As was earlier pointed out, horns represent nations and kingdoms. Those nations exercised certain powers over their inhabitants and others within their spheres of influence. From the rendering of horns in this instance, it is clear that the reference is akin to the power, influence, and strength of the nation. For the record has already declared that it was one beast (nation) and not two nations to be represented by the two horns. Notice also, that unlike the beast from the sea, the beast from the earth has no crowns upon its horns. This denotes the lack of kingly or ecclesiastical authority over the inhabitants of the new nation.

Nevertheless, John is in effect referring to the source of strength of this earth nation. These characteristics, quite accurately, identified this new nation, arising from the earth, to be the United States of America. And where does the power and strength of America lie? It is in her Constitution. America's strength lies in her people who operate under the precepts of what James Madison calls 'The sacred ark of the people's covenant.' The very first amendment of the U.S. Constitution reads thus, "Congress shall make no law, respecting the establishment of religion or prohibiting the free exercise thereof, or abridging the freedom of speech, or of the press; or the right of the people peaceably to assembly and to petition the government for a redress of grievances." More than anything else, this is what gives power and strength to the American ideal. It is the very foundation of the American experience. This is what is symbolized by the two horns of Revelation 13:11—Separation of church and state thus allowing civil and religious liberties.

On one hand there is the guarantee of religious freedom. Those that fled the persecuting power of the first beast (the Papacy) came to a land where they can worship God according to the dictates of their own consciences. Politician and educator, Edward Everett, in a speech made at Plymouth, Maine on December 22, 1824 declared, "Did they look for a retired spot, inoffensive for its obscurity, and safe in its remoteness, where the little church of Leyden might enjoy the freedom of conscience? Behold the might over which, in peaceful conquest, victory without strife, they have borne the banner of the cross." This is a conclusive and irrefutable interpretation of John's dream. Religious Liberty is one of the foundational pillars of our nation, the United States of America. Thus John symbolizes it as one of the horns on the lamb-like beast rising up out of the earth. It is one of the two sources of power of the American experiment. The other horn, or source of power, is equally important. It represents the other source of America's strength. In it is symbolized the other great foundational principle of these United States- Republicanism. This idea suggests a government for the people, of the people, and by the people. It further guarantees the respect of minority rights within the context of majority rule.

Even though America has not always lived up to that ideal, it is a principle, nevertheless, in stark contrast to the lands of Europe from which so many fled to make America their home. The idea of a country without a king and a church without a pope was one for which men and women were willing to risk all their lives and all earthly possessions. The Constitution of the United States, with its principle of civil and religious liberties, afforded the immigrants of Europe just that. Article IV Section 4 of the U.S. constitution reads, "The United States shall guarantee to every state in this union a Republican form of government" Article VI reads, "No religious test shall ever be required as a qualification to any office of public trust under the United States."

These revolutionary concepts were uniquely American. They were conceived and implemented as bulwarks against the incursion of Papal principles into the new nation. It was as if Omnipotence had ordained the United States of America to be a divine oasis in His grand plan for the redemption of men's souls.

But what John sees afterward is quite shocking. He states that this nation, the United States of America, the lamb-like beast with two horns, will one day speak like a dragon. He continues, "And he (America, the lamb- like beast) exerciseth all the power of the first beast before him, and causeth the earth and them which dwell therein to worship the first beast, whose deadly wound was healed" (Revelation 13: 12). The dragon is Satan, the devil (Revelation 12:9) from which the Bible declares that the sea beast, the Papacy, gets its power and authority (Revelation 13:2).

Amazingly, the prophecy foretells that the United States will not only speak like the dragon; (repudiate its Constitutional principles, and enact laws that deprive its citizens of their God given and constitutionally decreed freedoms) but it will force the entire world to worship the Papacy. This is indeed amazing, shocking and unbelievable, but true. God's Word says it, and God's Word is truth. (John 17:17). John continues to write of America, the lamb-like beast, "And he doeth great wonders so that he makes fire come down from heaven on the earth in the sight of men" (Revelation 13:13). Jesus Christ, when relating the events that would precede His Second Coming, predicted, "There shall arise false Christs, and false prophets, and shall show great signs and wonders, insomuch that if it were possible, they shall deceive the very elect" (Matthew 24:24).

Now, John declares that such miracles will take place in the period of America's leadership of the world as she forces men and women to worship the pope of Rome through the forced observance of Sunday sacredness. To this end, these miracles are wrought. John explains, "and deceives them that dwell on the earth by the means of those miracles which he had power to do in the sight of the first beast (the Papacy) saying to them that dwell on the earth, that they should make an image to the beast (first beast/Papacy) which had the wound by the sword and did live" (Revelation 13:14).

The apostle Paul, in describing Jesus, expresses this thought, "Who (Jesus) being the brightness of His glory, and the expressed image of His (God the Father) person" (Hebrews 1:3). Jesus confirms, "I and My Father are One...If you have seen Me you have seen the Father" (John 10:30, John 14:9). Here, both Jesus Christ and the apostle Paul are making it very clear that Jesus is like unto His Father. He is the express image of His Father. In similar fashion, John reports that the United States of America will become in character, exactly like the Papacy. That is what is meant by making an image to the first beast, the Papacy. And what is the Papacy? It is the amalgamation of pagan religious doctrines, sprinkled with enough Christianity to make it appear Christian. Those dogmas are then enforced and upheld by the power of the state under the influence of the church. That is the historic character of the Papacy. It is what the apostle John says that America will become.

The call for enforced Sunday sacredness is rapidly gaining traction. America, the prophet foretells, will eventually move from its position of religious freedom and political openness, to one of religious intolerance and ruthless political and civil suppression. It will become exactly like the Papacy of old. In fact, it would be the Papacy, through her agents, that would skillfully bring this about.

Ellen G. White, the eloquent nineteenth century Christian writer, prophesies, "By the decree enforcing the institution of the Papacy in violation of the law of God, our nation will disconnect herself fully from righteousness. When Protestantism shall stretch her hand across the gulf to grasp the hand of the Roman power, when she shall reach over the abyss to clasp hands with spiritualism, when under the influence of this threefold union, our country shall repudiate (abandon) every principle of its Constitution as a Protestant and Republican government, and shall make provision for the propagation of papal falsehoods and delusions, then we may know that the time has come for the marvelous working of Satan and that the end is near" (Testimonies for the Church, Ellen G. White, Volume 5, page 451).

But America, John says, will do much more than become like the Papacy. He moves on, "And he (America) had power to give life into the image of the beast, that the image of the beast should both speak, and cause that as many as would not worship the image of the beast should be killed" (Revelation 13:15). As the Papacy was described as having worldwide power and influence so does America today. That power and influence coupled with a spirit of religious intolerance and political repression will be developed into what John term 'Image of the Beast'.

In its position as the world's dominant military and police force; America will not only lead in legislating oppressive religious laws in accordance with Papal dogmas and doctrines; but it will help ensure worldwide Papal domination. John is warning us that disobedience to those worldwide decrees will result in imprisonment, deprivation, and death. At the very core of that forced worship, John declares, will be the 'Mark of the Beast'. The point has already been made as to what the Mark of the Beast is—-Sunday sacredness. John's prophecy continues: "And he (America) causes all, both small and great, rich and poor, free and bond, to receive a mark in their right hand, or in their foreheads…and that no man may buy or sell, save that he has the mark or the name of the beast, or the number of his name" (Revelation 13:17).

Speculations and opinions abound about the matters of the mark, the image, the name, and the number of the beast. But you need not be deceived. We have clearly established from historical records, Biblical prophecy, and Papal decrees what is the beast and what is its mark. The mark is neither a bar code nor a computer chip to be implanted in the forehead or right hand. It is not our computer. The mark is, as is emphatically stated and confirmed by the beast itself, Sunday sacredness. This is in contradiction to a free choice for God's blessed Sabbath-day. According to John's prophecy, the United States will enact laws (speak) and enforce (cause) men everywhere to accept Sunday as a sacred day of worship in honor and recognition of the Pope of Rome as the Vicar of Christ on the earth.

The resurgence, growth, and eventual domination of America by the Papacy began in earnest with the election of Pope Pius XI in 1922. In the classic, Rome Stoops to Conquer, by E. Boyd Barrett, a renowned Jesuit scholar, we discover the following: "Pius is well aware that the Catholic Church can never hope again to dominate the civilized world until America kneels, beaten and penitent at her feet...In teaching American Catholics this new phase of Catholicism, this active phase, and in sanctifying it with his blessings, Pius X1 rendered inevitable many significant changes in the life course of this nation" (Rome Stoops To Conquer, page 4). The new phase here refers to an aggressive, well defined and organized plan to control all aspects of American life. As we look around the American landscape today, no one can doubt that Pius' vision and initiatives to make America Catholic have been resoundingly successful.

Catholicism, through her dedicated sons and daughters, is in control of the media, business, government, the judiciary, politics and religion. So successful is Rome's plan for America that we find former president, George W. Bush admonishing the nation to follow the teachings of the Roman Catholic Church. He visited the Vatican to present to the late Pope John Paul II the Medal of Honor. This is the highest recognition our nation can give to an individual. What a pitiful sight it was to see three living American presidents paying homage to the Papacy by kneeling before the dead body of Pope John Paul II.

Pius' aim for America was and still is the centerpiece of the Vatican's strategy for world domination. Professor E. Boyd Bartlett continues, "Though Pius has little liking for our wicked ways and our heresies, he sees in us the nation that counts for most in the world today-the nation of the future. We are rich, young, strong, and our life is before us as a nation... He would have us, he needs us; he means to have us. He believes that the destiny of the church will be fulfilled in America and that with the spiritual conquest of America, the world dominion of the church will be regained" (ibid. 259).

When Pius' vision for a Catholic America is fully manifested, then the church's mark of authority, Sunday sacredness, according to God's Word, will be forcibly and rigidly enforced. But God has already given us a sacred day of rest. He gave it to us from creation. It is His holy and blessed Sabbath-day (Genesis 2:2, 3). He has not changed it, nor has he given any man or organization the permission or authority to do so. The U.S. Constitution, with its inherent principles of civil and religious liberties, though used positively when it advances her program for its destruction, is an innate abhorrence to popery. The Papacy's longstanding position is that of hatred for the concepts of liberty and freedom that have found their finest hour in the American experience. Pope Pius VII exclaimed, "It was declared that all religious persuasions should be free and their worship publicly exercised. But, we have rejected this article as contrary to the canons and councils of the first Catholic Church" (Encyclical, 1808).

Ironically, every United States president, since Ronald Reagan, has made the accommodation of the Papacy a key component of the presidency. Knowingly or unknowingly, our presidents have been moving the country steadily towards Papal rule. Former president George W. Bush urged the nation to follow the teachings of Pope John Paul II in his remarks of a monument in honor of the late pope. Pope John Paul II responded with great jubilation: "We will come to view this as our little Vatican in the United States." To some Americans, this seems commendable and laudable; but, to many, it is immensely disturbing and disheartening. America was born as a Protestant nation. We are supposed to be protesting against the errors of Romanism. As a Protestant people, we should be holding fast to the Bible and the Bible only.

Romanism and Americanism cannot exist side by side. One has to obliterate the other. Under the right set of circumstances, most likely characterized by confusion and chaos, the Papal solution of Sunday sacredness will be proposed as the solution. The evidence suggests that such is already the case. The current pope, Francis, has in fact proposed such in his encyclical, Laudato SI'. According to God's Word, Sunday sacredness will be legislated and ultimately implemented. The citizenry, having disconnected themselves from God, by rejecting His Holy Sabbath-day, will force their petitions for Sunday sacredness. They will see it as a panacea for America and the world's problems. Moves in that direction are well under way.

Considering the current make-up of the United States Congress, the passage and enforcement of Sunday as a national day of rest will be easily accomplished. The Pew Forum on Religion and Public Life, a leading research organization on religious trends in the United States, offers these statistics on the religious composition of the United States Congress.

House of Representative	Senate
Catholics 30%	24%
Protestants 57% (56.6% Sunday Keeper	57%
Jews 7.3%	12%

(Source: Pew Research Forum)

Regardless of the pretext used to pass such a law, the fact remains that it will be in violation of the First Amendment of the U.S. Constitution which specifically prohibits the establishment of any religion. If challenged, the U.S. Supreme Court, with six of nine justices being Catholic, will more likely than not uphold it. The concept of a day of rest is rooted in the Judeo/Christian religion. That day of rest, based on the Bible, is God's holy Sabbath-day, the seventh day of the week (Genesis 2:2, 3; Exodus 20; 8-11). Sunday sacredness is blatant and open rebellion to God's command. God offers a choice. The devil forces his will. This is a simple fact of life which most seem not to realize. To follow the pope of Rome on the matter of the Sabbath is tantamount to rejecting the God of creation. The issue is beyond the days. It is a question of who one worships—the God of creation or the Pope of Rome.

How then will men receive the Mark of the Beast? It is a choice one has to make. It is a decision that will determine ones eternal destiny. God does not force anyone to honor Him by keeping holy His Sabbath day. When this oppressive, worldwide decree is enacted and the evidence of God's true Sabbath is presented, as it is in this volume; then all will be required to make their choice either for God's Sabbath or the tradition of men. There is no middle ground. It is either God's holy Sabbath or man's tradition of Sunday. Everyone will have to choose either the seventh-day as ordained by God or the first day as instituted by man. Upon enactment and enforcement of the false Sabbath, one will receive the mark of the beast by purposely rejecting God's seventh-day Sabbath whilst consciously choosing to venerate Sunday in obedience to the Papacy.

Jesus beckons us, "If you love me, keep my commandments" (John 14:15). That includes the Sabbath commandment (Exodus 20:8–11). In the very words of God's commands rest the power to obey that which He commands. By faith you can and must obey.

The impending worldwide decree to enforce Sunday sacredness, with America as the chief enforcer, is not so far-fetched at all. Very soon after America's birth as a nation, the spirit of Romanism began to raise its ugly head. Those who had fled religious persecution to find refuge in America attempted, with some success, to do exactly that which they ran away from. The history of the Colonial period with the Puritan Pilgrims is a prime example. People were punished and killed for not abiding by the rules of the church dominated colonies.

The same spirit was manifested with regards to Sunday sacredness in more recent history. Following the California gold rush of the 1840s that state passed a law in 1859, forbidding business to open on Sunday. By 1882 more than 1600 violators were arrested. So heated was the issue of Sunday sacredness, that it found its way on the platform of both political parties in the general election of 1882. In 1885 several persons were also arrested, jailed and/or fined in the state of Arkansas for violating that state's Sunday blue law, which prohibited work on Sunday. In 1889, both the state Supreme Court and U.S. Circuit Court upheld the conviction of a Tennessee man who violated that state's Sunday closing law.

Also, in 1889, the issue of Sunday sacredness was the substance of two bills introduced in the U.S. Senate by Senator H.W. Blair of New Hampshire. The first bill, calling for the promotion of Sunday as a national day of rest, referred to Sunday as "The Lord's Day." The other bill called for a constitutional amendment requiring the public schools to teach "the principle of the Christian Religion". That principle, as some perceived it, was honoring Sunday as the emblem of the nation's Christian identity. The same spirit, of state legislated morality is alive and growing in the nation today. Of course, the efforts in the 1800s, failed to legislate a National Sunday Law. However, we are now at a point in the history of the United States, where a legislated National Day of Rest (Sunday), is a real possibility. In fact, according to God's Word, it is a sure reality (Revelation 13:11-17).

As the nation experiences accelerating moral decay, unrelenting sexual promiscuity, increased violence, religious indifference, threats of terrorism, deeper discussions on climate change, and economic uncertainty, the calls are mounting to return to God by making Sunday a holy day. Organizations such as the Moral Majority, the Christian Coalition, National Back to Church Sunday, and the Lord's Day Alliance, among others, are joining forces with the Papacy that will bring about legislation for Sunday as a national day of rest. Their actions, well intentioned as they might seem, are not only a violation of our constitutional principles but an affront to the God of Creation. They are verily a fulfillment of John's prophecy.

God has given us His day of rest from creation. That day is His Holy Sabbath-day (Genesis 2:2, 3). He has sent His prophets to teach us about it, and has given Jesus Christ as our example to honor it. He wants our free choice not our forced worship. He is calling His people to come back and worship Him as He desires (Revelation 14:6, 7).

So called religious leaders are in effect refusing God's offer of free choice and are opting for forced religious dogmas. They are attempting to establish their own standard of righteousness by elevating Sunday to take the place of God's Holy Sabbath. Jesus warned the religious leaders of His day, "This people honor Me with their lips, but their heart is far from Me…Howbeit in vain do they worship Me, teaching for doctrines the commandments of men…For laying aside the commandment of God, ye hold the tradition of men" (Mark 7:6-8). With regards to God's Sabbath, this is exactly what men and women, professing to be Christians, are doing in the exhalation of Sunday. Jesus asks, "And why call ye Me Lord, Lord, and do not the things which I say? (Luke 6:46)

America is a nation that is abundantly blessed with God's bounties, including an overflowing of His Word. Too many people, claiming to belong to Him, are unfortunately choosing not only to follow men's traditions in the exaltation of Sunday; but also are seeking to move the whole nation to do likewise. This is deception of the highest order. The apostle Paul addresses the issue, "Because that, when they know God, they glorified Him not as God, neither were thankful; but became vain in their imaginations, and their foolish heart was darkened…professing themselves to be wise, they became fools" (Romans 1:21, 22). He continues, "And with all deceivableness of unrighteousness in them that perish; because they received not the love of the truth, that they might be saved…And for this cause God shall send them strong delusions that they should believe a lie: that they all might be damned, who believe not the truth, but had pleasure in unrighteousness" (2 Thessalonians 2:10-12).

How sad for a people who have been given so much by Almighty God. As America continues her march toward tearing down God's holy law, whilst uplifting the traditions of the man of sin in its place, great tribulation and destruction will befall the nation along with the rest of the world. As the nation, under the pretense of greater security, repudiates the principles of its constitution, it will be swept swiftly under total control of Romanism and horrible cruelties will follow. Some, however, will be faithful to the God of creation. Even in such a time as these, God's character will be vindicated by those, who in the face of deprivation and death, will uphold His holy Sabbath-day. This has always been the history of God's people. Not unlike Luther, Wycliffe, Calvin, Jerome, Elijah, Shadrach, Meshach, Abednego and multitudes of others, God's true disciples will stand, even unto death, in this imminent crisis. The question is: will you be one of them?

CHAPTER 7

The Final Movements

On May 24th, 2015 Pope Francis released his long awaited, controversial, and much debated encyclical on the environment. The central issue being addressed is the threat of global warming to the environment and its impact on the poor, the family, and the world's economy. Undergirding his thesis is humanity's need to protect and take care of creation. Before its "official" release, the world was presented with a 'leaked' version that accelerated discussions on the issue. Religionists, politicians, and scientists were offering their take on the impact of Francis' encyclical on the climate change debate.

Jeb Bush, Roman Catholic and then Republican candidate for the presidency, disagreed with his pope's position on climate change. He declared, "I hope I'm not going to get castigated for saying this by my priest back home...religion ought to be about making us better as people and less about things that end up getting into the political realm." Those words are eerily reminiscent of the late John F. Kennedy's declaration to a gathering of Protestant ministers in Houston, Texas in September, 1960 as he sought to convince the electorate that as a Roman Catholic, he will not run the country according to the teachings of his church, but rather on the basis of the country's Constitution. He was cruelly assassinated in Dallas, Texas before the on-looking world three years later.

Other declared Republican candidates have sounded similar sentiments. Rick Santorum, also Roman Catholic, shared his thoughts on Francis' encyclical. He pleaded with his pontiff, "Leave science to the scientists." Perhaps Bush, Santorum and the rest of the world need to be reminded that Francis, the head of the Papacy, is not merely a religious leader, but also a political head of state ruling over more than one billion citizens in every country on planet earth. The American ideal of separation of church and state has zero value in that realm. This is the perspective from which Francis operates. Wake up America.

On the other side of the political divide, Democratic Vice President and Roman Catholic, Joseph Biden, certainly agreed with his pope on climate change. Invoking Francis' encyclical at a clean air conference at the White House, he stated, "Usually encyclicals are only issued on what the church thinks are incredibly important initiatives...this doesn't only have a moral component to it, it has a security component to it, as well as it has an economic component to it." Biden's view underscores the broad implications of Francis' letter. It, in essence, is about more than protecting the environment and caring for the poor and disenfranchised; but rather yet another of Francis' tactics in his church's long standing strategy to change the political climate of the world.

In his book, Keys of This Blood, Malachi Martin, the late Jesuit scholar and expert commentator on the operations and aims of the Papacy, revealed that there was a three way struggle for world domination. He identified the players in that competition as Communism, Globalism (Capitalism), and Catholicism. Since the publication of his book in 1990, one of those competitors has been effectively neutralized. Time Magazine's cover headline glared: "HOLY ALLIANCE... how Reagan and the pope conspired to assist Poland's solidarity movement and hasten the demise of Communism"(Time, February 24, 1992).

The ensuing article stated, "On June 7, 1982, Reagan and John Paul met for 50 minutes at the Vatican. During that conversation, the plot was hatched to eliminate communism. In that meeting, Reagan and the Pope agreed to undertake a clandestine campaign to hasten the dissolution of the communist regime, declares Richard Allen, Reagan's first National Security adviser, 'This was one of the great secret alliances of all time" (Time Magazine, February 24, 1992, page 28).

There are now two remaining players in that competition for world domination, Catholicism and Globalism fueled by Capitalist America. Malachi Martin concluded, "That being the case, it would appear inescapable that their competition will end up in confrontation. It is not too much to say in fact, that the chosen purpose of John

Paul's Pontificate, the engine that drives his papal grand policy and that determines his day- to- day, year- to- year strategies is to be the victor in that competition, well underway" (Keys of this Blood, page 15).

John Paul II has now passed off the scene, but the Papacy's objective, as evidenced by Francis' political and religious maneuverings, remains the same. The sad commentary is that whilst this phenomenon is well understood by the agents of Rome, it is totally oblivious to most Americans. Francis continues to relentlessly wage the battle for Papal domination, attacking the unsuspecting competition from within. His encyclical on climate change is simply one giant step in that direction. His address to the joint session of Congress in September 24, 2016, further decrying the evils of capitalism, is yet another. As Catholicism, with Francis at the helm, is being strengthened and widely perceived as good for humanity's wellbeing; America, the engine that drives Globalism, is becoming weaker and weaker through the attacks on the foundational principles of her Constitution, primarily the concept of separation of church and state. What we are experiencing in America today is a rather rapid, though stealthy, implementation of Papal rule built upon its foundational tenet of unification of church and state. Popery is antagonistic to the American system of justice and liberty for all.

Francis continually insists that the panacea for the world's problems rests with his church's version of morality and spirituality, at the very foundation of which is Sunday sacredness. His ultimate aim is to have the nations of the world recognize this and institute it into their laws. This is rapidly happening across Europe through the agency of the European Sunday Alliance, an organization immensely supported by the papacy.

The Associated Press recently reported, "Pope Francis lamented the abandoning of the traditionally Christian practice of not working on Sundays, saying it has a negative impact on families and friendships." He says that spending Sundays with family and friends is an "ethical choice" for faithful and non-faithful alike... preserving the special character of Sunday as the Lord's Day — even civilly where possible." His predecessor, Benedict XI asserted, "At a time when creation seems to be endangered in so many ways through human activity, we should consciously accept this dimension of Sunday, too...It is necessary to promote reflection and efforts at reconciling the demands and the periods of work with those of the family and to recover the true meaning of the feast, especially on Sunday, the weekly Easter, the day of the lord, and the day of man, the day of the family, of the community, and of solidarity" (Zenith. org, Sept. 26 2010). A leading church publication of its time stated, "Sunday is our mark of authority...the church is above the Bible, and the transference of Sabbath is proof of that fact. (Catholic Record, Sept 1, 1923).

Despite the differing opinions on Francis' position on climate change, one thing is for sure-almost all (Revelation 13:8) are coming together on Rome's proposition for Sunday sacredness, ostensibly to save not only the environment and take care of creation, but also to strengthen the family, and by extension, society as a whole. Sunday sacredness will bridge the divide on climate change.

But herein lies the potential for greatest conflict of all. Relative to creation, the Bible teaches that the God of creation has already given humanity a day of rest and worship. It is the 7th day and not the 1st. It reads, "Thus the heavens and the earth were finished, and all the host of them. And on the seventh day God ended his work which he had made; and he rested on the seventh day from all his work which he had made And God blessed the seventh day, and sanctified it: because that in it he had rested from all his work which God created and made" (Exodus 2:1-3). .

Contrary to the Papal call for legislated decrees for Sunday sacredness, the Creator sends out a love message in the image of an angel with a loud voice, lovingly beckoning all humanity today: "Fear God, and give glory to him; for the hour of his judgment is come: and worship him that made heaven, and earth, and the sea, and the fountains of waters" (Revelation 14:7).

Ultimately, all will have to take a stand, not on climate change; but either on Papal tradition of Sunday sacredness or the Seventh-day Sabbath of Creator God. Where will you stand?

The year 1965 marked the completion of the Vatican Council II, the Roman Catholic Church's initiative to develop and implement a comprehensive strategy by which it would bring the entire world under its control. The underlining theme of that ongoing strategy is unity of all religions and governments. One of its main objectives was to bring the 'separated brethren' (heretics before Vatican II) back to the Catholic fold. Today, looking over the religious and political landscape, one can hardly deny the success of Rome's strategy for world domination as outlined in Vatican Council II.

It has been fifty years now and the current Jesuit Pope, Francis, has declared that this is the year of the Jubilee. In his recent encyclical, LAUDATO SI', he invokes the Biblical passages of the Old Testament referring to Sabbath, the Sabbatical Year and the Jubilee. He writes, "We see this, for example, in the law of the Sabbath. On the seventh day, God rested from all his work. He commanded Israel to set aside each seventh day as a day of rest, a Sabbath, (cf. Gen 2:2-3; Ex 16:23; 20:10). Similarly, every seven years, a sabbatical year was set aside for Israel, a complete rest for the land (cf. Lev 25:1-4), when sowing was forbidden and one reaped only what was necessary to live on and to feed one's household (cf. Lev 25:4-6). Finally, after seven weeks of years, which is to say forty-nine years, the Jubilee was celebrated as a year of general forgiveness and "liberty throughout the land for all its inhabitants" (cf. Lev 25:10). This law came about as an attempt to ensure balance and fairness in their relationships with others and with the land on which they lived and worked." (LAUDATO SI', Section 71).

His invocation of and subsequent re-contextualization of these Biblical concepts are presented as the foundation upon which his prescription for solving the world's problems is built. Jehovah God intended that His Sabbath, the Sabbatical Year, and the Biblical Jubilee would remind His people that He is their Creator, that they are stewards and that they ought to conduct themselves and manage the earth in a manner that would glorify Him and benefit all humanity. These are prescribed as times of justice, mercy, equity, rest for humanity and the earth, and reflection upon Him who gave it all to us. Francis, in his encyclical, offers his versions of these concepts as solutions to take care of the poor, stop ozone depletion, and remedy the world's economic woes. In doing so, he is in fact attempting to take the place of God; for it is the God of Creation who gave us the Sabbath, the Sabbatical Year, and the Jubilee.

The Sabbatical year (every seventh year) and the Jubilee (every fiftieth year) are extrapolations of the Seventh-day Sabbath given to humanity at creation (Genesis 2:1-3). It is not a Jewish Sabbath. It is the Creator's Sabbath, the day of rest, bequeathed to all humanity. In giving humanity this sanctuary in time, Jehovah God intended that all would remember Him as their Creator, the One upon whom they depend for their every need. The Sabbatical Year and the Jubilee were instituted to further impress our minds of God's creative and sustaining power. The Jewish nation was the instrument in God's hands used to teach this most vital lesson to all mankind. His servant Isaiah declared, "And he said, It is a light thing that thou shouldest be my servant to raise up the tribes of Jacob, and to restore the preserved of Israel: I will also give thee for a light to the Gentiles, that thou mayest be my salvation unto the end of the earth (Isaiah 49:6). God instructed His servant Moses and reminds us today, "Remember the Sabbath day, to keep it holy. Six days shalt thou labour, and do all thy work: But the seventh day is the Sabbath of the Lord thy God: in it thou shalt not do any work, thou, nor thy son, nor thy daughter, thy manservant, nor thy maidservant, nor thy cattle, nor thy stranger that is within thy gates: For in six days the Lord made heaven and earth, the sea, and all that in them is, and rested the seventh day: wherefore the Lord blessed the Sabbath day, and hallowed it" (Exodus 20:8-11).

For the Sabbatical year, based upon the seventh-day Sabbath, God further admonished Moses, "Six years thou shalt sow thy field, and six years thou shalt prune thy vineyard, and gather in the fruit thereof; But in the seventh year shall be a Sabbath of rest unto the land, a Sabbath for the Lord: thou shalt neither sow thy field, nor prune thy vineyard" (Leviticus 25:3-4). Regarding the Jubilee, the fiftieth year, Creator God again directed Moses, "And thou shalt number seven Sabbaths of years unto thee, seven times seven years; and the space of the seven Sabbaths of years shall be unto thee forty and nine years. Then shalt thou cause the trumpet of the Jubilee to sound on the tenth day of the seventh month, in the Day of Atonement shall ye make the trumpet sound throughout all your land. And ye shall hallow the fiftieth year, and proclaim liberty throughout all the land unto all the inhabitants thereof: it shall be a Jubilee unto you; and ye shall return every man unto his possession, and ye shall return every man unto his family "(Leviticus 25:8-10).

Francis' subtle, yet blatant usurpation of the God of Creation is evident in his encyclical. He states, "On Sunday, our participation in the Eucharist has special importance. Sunday, like the Jewish Sabbath, is meant to be a day which heals our relationships with God, with ourselves, with others and with the world. Sunday is the day of the Resurrection, the "first day" of the new creation, whose first fruits are the Lord's risen humanity, the pledge of the final transfiguration of all created reality. It also proclaims "man's eternal rest in God" (LAUDATO SI', Section 237). How can a mere human being transfer the meaning, sacredness, and sanctity of God's Sabbath, the 7th day of the week, to Sunday, the first, and by extension relegate the blessings of the Creator's Jubilee to one he and his church have invented? But this is indeed what Francis is doing in LAUDATO SI'.

Kevin P. Emmert, in his June 19, 2015, article, Why the Pope Is Going Green, appearing in Christianity Today Online, puts Francis' encyclical in perspective when he observes, "The encyclical, however, is far more than a doomsday letter or a how-to of environmental care. Underlying the warnings and prescriptions, he offers a theology of creation that emphasizes how, by God's design; human beings and the created world are deeply connected. If we understand this, Francis says, it can change the way we relate to God, to one another, and creation." But we must relate to God, each other, and to creation based on God's prescription, His Ten Commandments (Exodus 20:2-17), and not Francis' LAUDATO SI' which prescribes Sunday sacredness and the Eucharist in its place. Will you rest your hopes on the word of Creator God or upon the sinking sand of Francis' empty promises? The choice is yours to make.

Francis is not God, Sunday is not God's Sabbath and the 50th anniversary of Vatican Council II is not His Jubilee. The Eucharist and Sunday sacredness are inventions of his church and are patently opposed to the word of God. The Bible plainly teaches, "So Christ was once offered to bear the sins of many; and unto them that look for him shall he appear the second time without sin unto salvation" (Hebrews 9:28, 10:14). Contrariwise, the Eucharist is thus defined: "By the consecration the transubstantiation of the bread and wine into the Body and Blood of Christ is brought about. Under the consecrated species of bread and wine Christ himself, living and glorious, is present in a true, real, and substantial manner: his Body and his Blood, with his soul and his divinity (Catechism of the Catholic Church, 1413).

Observing the 7th day Sabbath, the Sabbatical year and the Jubilee are acts of worship due only to Creator God. We honor Him by obeying His commandments. Sunday sacredness, the Eucharist, and imbibing a false jubilee are acts of obedience to and worship of another power. Both the prophets Daniel in the Old Testament (Daniel 2, 7, 8 & 11) and John (Revelation 13, 17&18) in the New, clearly identify this power. The Apostle Paul speaks of it thus, "Let no man deceive you by any means: for that day shall not come, except there come a falling away first, and that man of sin be revealed, the son of perdition; Who opposeth and exalteth himself above all that is called God, or that is worshipped; so that he as God sitteth in the temple of God, shewing himself that he is God" (2 Thessalonians 2:3-4). The Protestant Reformers were all in agreement. It is none other than the Roman Papacy. Both history and Scripture testify of it as one taking the prerogatives of God, seeking to change God's law, persecuting God's true followers, and claiming to take the place of God on earth.

The promises of Francis, its current head, will not bring peace, justice, equity and rest; but rather usher in unmitigated chaos, bloody repression, and ultimately total destruction. The prophet Daniel reveals, "And at that time shall Michael stand up, the great prince which standeth for the children of thy people: and there shall be a time of trouble, such as never was since there was a nation even to that same time: and at that time thy people shall be delivered, every one that shall be found written in the book" (Daniel 12:1). Then begins God's Jubilee (1 Thessalonians 4:16-18; Revelation 20:4).

Quite unlike Francis' prescription for harmony, equity and security, Creator God warns of a world that is swiftly travelling towards its appointment with a dismal destiny. The ancient seer, Jeremiah, describes it thus, "I beheld the earth, and, lo, it was without form, and void; and the heavens, and they had no light. I beheld the mountains, and, lo, they trembled, and all the hills moved lightly. I beheld, and, lo, there was no man, and all the birds of the heavens were fled. I beheld, and, lo, the fruitful place was a wilderness, and all the cities thereof were broken down at the presence of the Lord, and by his fierce anger. For thus hath the Lord said, the whole land shall be desolate; yet will I not make a full end. For this shall the earth mourn, and the heavens above be black; because I have spoken it, I have purposed it, and will not repent, neither will I turn back from it" (Jeremiah 4:23-28). And why would this be? His fellow seer, Isaiah, who is in total agreement (Isaiah 24:1-4) answers, "The earth also is defiled under the inhabitants thereof; because they have transgressed the laws, changed the ordinance, broken the everlasting covenant" (Isaiah 24:5).

Contrary to God's loving call to worship Him as Creator by honoring His blessed Sabbath day (Ex 20:8-11; Revelation 14:6-7); Francis' promises are built upon another foundation: "Christians will naturally strive to ensure that "civil legislation" respects their duty to keep Sunday holy" (Section 67, Dies Domini, July 7, 1998).

The strategy for establishment of Sunday sacredness, as a means for achieving world domination, was adopted several centuries ago at the Council of Trent. At this Counter Reformation Council which explored ways of bringing the heretics back to the mother church, Archbishop of Reggio, Gaspar Ricculli de Fasso, concluded, "The Protestants claim to stand upon the written word only. They profess to hold the Scripture alone as the standard of faith. They justify their revolt by the plea that the Church has apostatized from the written word and follows tradition. Now the Protestant claim that they stand upon the written word only, is not true. Their profession of holding the Scripture alone as the standard of faith is false. PROOF: The written word explicitly enjoins the observance of the seventh day as the Sabbath. They do not observe the seventh day but reject it. If they do truly hold the scripture alone as their standard, they would be observing the seventh day as is enjoined in the Scripture throughout. Yet they not only reject the observance of the Sabbath enjoined in the written word, but they have adopted and do practice the observance of Sunday, for which they have only the tradition of the Church. Consequently the claim of 'Scripture alone as the standard,' fails; and the doctrine of 'Scripture and tradition' as essential, is fully established, the Protestants themselves being judges." (J. H. Holtzman, Canon and Tradition, published in Ludwigsburg, Germany, in 1859, page 263, and Archbishop of Reggio's address in the 17th session of the Council of Trent, Jan. 18, 1562, in Mansi SC, Vol. 33, cols. 529, 530).

It was upon this declaration that the Council found its most viable instrument against the Protestant Reformation. Its success is undeniable and is being used most effectively to shortly force the entire world to honor the papacy as the supreme ruler of the world.

Top Vatican adviser Jeffrey Sachs forewarned that when Pope Francis visits the United States in September, 2015, he will directly challenge the "American idea" of God-given rights embodied in the Declaration of Independence. Sachs, a special advisor to the United Nations and director of the Earth Institute at Columbia

University writes in the Jesuit publication, *America*: "America is 'a society in thrall' to the idea of unalienable rights to life, liberty, and the pursuit of happiness. But the "urgent core of Francis' message" will be to challenge this "American idea" by "proclaiming that the path to happiness lies not solely or mainly through the defense of rights but through the exercise of virtues, most notably justice and charity."(Western Journalism, May 19, 2015). It is clear that destroying the American Constitution, which guarantees the freedom of choice in religious matters, and substituting Papal dogmas, which forces the conscience in its place, is Francis' ultimate objective.

It is indeed a sad commentary on the American experience that the very body, which in its infancy, established laws specifically opposed to Papal rule; now in its maturity, has invited the Roman Pontiff to instruct it that the ideas of the Founding Fathers must be repudiated. The Founding Fathers would be indescribably appalled could they have witnessed such a retrogression to that which they sacrificed their all.

The nations of the world have agreed with the pope that we do have a climate problem. At the Climate Change conference in France, from 30 November to 12 December 2015, an agreement was signed by all 196 attending nations acknowledging that the world does indeed have a climate problem. Pope Francis, who aggressively urged the nations to make that agreement, had of course laid out the solution for the problem several months before in his encyclical, Laudato SI'. His solution—-Sunday sacredness.

His next move was to offer the world a door of mercy through which all must return to his church. He decreed that his 'door of mercy' closes on November 20, 2016. Question is, what happens after his door closes? The answer lies in his church's unchanged policies of the Dark Ages which led to the unmerciful slaughter of millions whose only crime was to choose Jesus as their only way of salvation, rather than the Pope of Rome and his church.

Jesus Christ is the Only Door. He declares, "Verily, verily, I say unto you, He that entereth not by the door into the sheepfold, but climbeth up some other way, the same is a thief and a robber. But he that entereth in by the door is the shepherd of the sheep. To him the porter openeth; and the sheep hear his voice: and he calleth his own sheep by name, and leadeth them out. And when he putteth forth his own sheep, he goeth before them, and the sheep follow him: for they know his voice…I am the door: by me if any man enter in, he shall be saved, and shall go in and out, and find pasture" (John 10:1-3, 9).

Rather than the panacea for humanity's problems, Francis' prescription of Sunday sacredness and return to his church for salvation is leading the world to the bottomless pit. The final movements will be rapid ones.

CHAPTER 8

Aims of the Papacy

omanism is now regarded by Protestants with far greater favor than in former years. In those countries where Catholicism is not in the ascendancy, and the papists are taking a conciliatory course in order to gain influence, there is an increasing indifference concerning the doctrines that separate the reformed churches from the papal hierarchy; the opinion is gaining ground that, after all, we do not differ so widely upon vital points as has been supposed, and that a little concession on our part will bring us into a better understanding with Rome. The time was when Protestants placed a high value upon the liberty of conscience which had been so dearly purchased. They taught their children to abhor popery and held that to seek harmony with Rome would be disloyalty to God. But how widely different are the sentiments now expressed!

The defenders of the Papacy declare that the church has been maligned, and the Protestant world are inclined to accept the statement. Many urge that it is unjust to judge the church of today by the abominations and absurdities that marked her reign during the centuries of ignorance and darkness. They excuse her horrible cruelty as the result of the barbarism of the times and plead that the influence of modern civilization has changed her sentiments.

Have these persons forgotten the claim of infallibility put forth for eight hundred years by this haughty power? So far from being relinquished, this claim was affirmed in the nineteenth century with greater positiveness than ever before. As Rome asserts that the "church never erred; nor will it, according to the Scriptures, ever err"

(John L. von Mosheim, Institutes of Ecclesiastical History, book 3, century II, part 2, chapter 2, section 9, note 17), how can she renounce the principles which governed her course in past ages?

The papal church will never relinquish her claim to infallibility. All that she has done in her persecution of those who reject her dogmas she holds to be right; and would she not repeat the same acts, should the opportunity be presented? Let the restraints now imposed by secular governments be removed and Rome be reinstated in her former power, and there would speedily be a revival of her tyranny and persecution.

A well-known writer speaks thus of the attitude of the papal hierarchy as regards freedom of conscience, and of the perils which especially threaten the United States from the success of her policy: "There are many who are disposed to attribute any fear of Roman Catholicism in the United States to bigotry or childishness. Such see nothing in the character and attitude of Romanism that is hostile to our free institutions, or find nothing portentous in its growth. Let us, then, first compare some of the fundamental principles of our government with those of the Catholic Church. "The Constitution of the United States guarantees liberty of conscience. Nothing is dearer or more fundamental. Pope Pius IX, in his Encyclical Letter of August 15, 1854, said: "The absurd and erroneous doctrines or ravings in defense of liberty of conscience are a most pestilential error—a pest, of all others, most to be dreaded in a state". The same pope, in his Encyclical Letter of December 8, 1864, anathematized "those who assert the liberty of conscience and of religious worship", also "all such as maintain that the church may not employ force."

The pacific tone of Rome in the United States does not imply a change of heart. She is tolerant where she is helpless. Says Bishop O'Connor: "Religious liberty is merely endured until the opposite can be carried into effect without peril to the Catholic world". The archbishop of St. Louis once said: "Heresy and unbelief are crimes; and in Christian countries, as in Italy and Spain, for instance, where all the people are Catholics, and where the Catholic religion is an essential part of the law of the land, they are punished as other crimes."

Every cardinal, archbishop, and bishop in the Catholic Church takes an oath of allegiance to the pope, in which occur the following words: "Heretics, schismatics, and rebels to our said lord (the pope), or his aforesaid successors, I will to my utmost persecute and oppose"

(Josiah Strong, *Our Country*, ch. 5, pars. 2-4). It is true that there are real Christians in the Roman Catholic communion. Thousands in that church are serving God according to the best light they have. They are not allowed access to His word, and therefore they do not discern the truth. They have never seen the contrast between a living heart service and a round of mere forms and ceremonies. God looks with pitying tenderness upon these souls, educated as they are in a faith that is delusive and unsatisfying. He will cause rays of light to penetrate the dense darkness that surrounds them. He will reveal to them the truth as it is in Jesus, and many will yet take their position with His people.

But Romanism as a system is no more in harmony with the gospel of Christ now than at any former period in her history. The Protestant churches are in great darkness, or they would discern the signs of the times. The Roman Church is far-reaching in her plans and modes of operation. She is employing every device to extend her influence and increase her power in preparation for a fierce and determined conflict to regain control of the world, to re-establish persecution, and to undo all that Protestantism has done. Catholicism is gaining ground upon every side. See the increasing number of her churches and chapels in Protestant countries. Look at the popularity of her colleges and seminaries in America, so widely patronized by Protestants. Look at the growth of ritualism in England and the frequent defections to the ranks of the Catholics. These things should awaken the anxiety of all who prize the pure principles of the gospel.

Protestants have tampered with and patronized popery; they have made compromises and concessions which Papists themselves are surprised to see and fail to understand. Men are closing their eyes to the real character of Romanism and the dangers to be apprehended from her supremacy. The people need to be aroused to resist the advances of this most dangerous foe to civil and religious liberty.

Many Protestants suppose that the Catholic religion is unattractive and that its worship is a dull, meaningless round of ceremony. Here they mistake. While Romanism is based upon deception, it is not a coarse and clumsy imposture. The religious service of the Roman Church is a most impressive ceremonial. Its gorgeous display and solemn rites fascinate the senses of the people and silence the voice of reason and of conscience. The eye is charmed. Magnificent churches, imposing processions, golden altars, jeweled shrines, choice paintings, and exquisite sculpture appeal to the love of beauty. The ear also is captivated. The music is unsurpassed. The rich notes of the deeptoned organ, blending with the melody of many voices as it swells through the lofty domes and pillared aisles of her grand cathedrals, cannot fail to impress the mind with awe and reverence.

This outward splendor, pomp, and ceremony, that only mocks the longings of the sin-sick soul, is an evidence of inward corruption. The religion of Christ needs not such attractions to recommend it. In the light shining from the cross, true Christianity appears so pure and lovely that no external decorations can enhance its true worth. It is the beauty of holiness, a meek and quiet spirit, which is of value with God.

Brilliancy of style is not necessarily an index of pure, elevated thought. High conceptions of art, delicate refinement of taste, often exist in minds that are earthly and sensual. They are often employed by Satan to lead men to forget the necessities of the soul, to lose sight of the future, immortal life, to turn away from their infinite Helper, and to live for this world alone.

A religion of externals is attractive to the unrenewed heart. The pomp and ceremony of the Catholic worship has a seductive, bewitching power, by which many are deceived; and they come to look upon the Roman Church as the very gate of heaven. None but those who have planted their feet firmly upon the foundation of truth, and whose hearts are renewed by the Spirit of God, are proof against her influence. Thousands who have not an experimental knowledge of Christ will be led to accept the forms of godliness without the power. Such a religion is just what the multitudes desire.

The church's claim to the right to pardon leads the Romanist to feel at liberty to sin; and the ordinance of confession, without which her pardon is not granted, tends also to give license to evil. He who kneels before fallen man, and opens in confession the secret thoughts and imaginations of his heart, is debasing his manhood and degrading every noble instinct of his soul. In unfolding the sins of his life to a priest,—an erring, sinful mortal, and too often corrupted with wine and licentiousness,—his standard of character is lowered, and he is defiled in consequence. His thought of God is degraded to the likeness of fallen humanity, for the priest stands as a representative of God. This degrading confession of man to man is the secret spring from which has flowed much of the evil that is defiling the world and fitting it for the final destruction. Yet to him who loves self-indulgence, it is more pleasing to confess to a fellow mortal than to open the soul to God. It is more palatable to human nature to do penance than to renounce sin; it is easier to mortify the flesh by sackcloth and nettles and galling chains than to crucify fleshly lusts. Heavy is the yoke which the carnal heart is willing to bear rather than bow to the yoke of Christ.

There is a striking similarity between the Church of Rome and the Jewish Church at the time of Christ's first advent. While the Jews secretly trampled upon every principle of the law of God, they were outwardly rigorous in the observance of its precepts, loading it down with exactions and traditions that made obedience painful and burdensome. As the Jews professed to revere the law, so do Romanists claim to reverence the cross. They exalt the symbol of Christ's sufferings, while in their lives they deny Him whom it represents.

Papists place crosses upon their churches, upon their altars, and upon their garments. Everywhere is seen the insignia of the cross. Everywhere it is outwardly honored and exalted. But the teachings of Christ are buried beneath a mass of senseless traditions, false interpretations, and rigorous exactions. The Saviour's words concerning the bigoted Jews, apply with still greater force to the leaders of the Roman Catholic Church: "They bind heavy burdens and grievous to be borne, and lay them on men's shoulders; but they themselves will not move them with one of their fingers." Matthew 23:4. Conscientious souls are kept in constant terror fearing the wrath of an offended God, while many of the dignitaries of the church are living in luxury and sensual pleasure.

The worship of images and relics, the invocation of saints, and the exaltation of the pope are devices of Satan to attract the minds of the people from God and from His Son. To accomplish their ruin, he endeavors to turn their attention from Him through whom alone they can find salvation. He will direct them to any object that can be substituted for the One who has said: "Come unto Me, all ye that labor and are heavy-laden, and I will give you rest" (Matthew 11:28).

It is Satan's constant effort to misrepresent the character of God, the nature of sin, and the real issues at stake in the great controversy. His sophistry lessens the obligation of the divine law and gives men license to sin. At the same time he causes them to cherish false conceptions of God so that they regard Him with fear and hate rather than with love. The cruelty inherent in his own character is attributed to the Creator; it is embodied in systems of religion and expressed in modes of worship. Thus the minds of men are blinded, and Satan secures them as his agents to war against God. By perverted conceptions of the divine attributes, heathen nations were led to believe human sacrifices necessary to secure the favor of Deity; and horrible cruelties have been perpetrated under the various forms of idolatry.

The Roman Catholic Church, uniting the forms of paganism and Christianity, and, like paganism, misrepresenting the character of God, has resorted to practices no less cruel and revolting. In the days of Rome's supremacy there were instruments of torture to compel assent to her doctrines. There was the stake for those who would not concede to her claims. There were massacres on a scale that will never be known until revealed in the judgment. Dignitaries of the church studied, under Satan their master, to invent means to cause the greatest possible torture and not end the life of the victim. In many cases the infernal process was repeated to the utmost limit of human endurance, until nature gave up the struggle, and the sufferer hailed death as a sweet release.

Such was the fate of Rome's opponents. For her adherents she had the discipline of the scourge, of famishing hunger, of bodily austerities in every conceivable, heart-sickening form. To secure the favor of Heaven, penitents violated the laws of God by violating the laws of nature. They were taught to sunder the ties which He has formed to bless and gladden man's earthly sojourn. The churchyard contains millions of victims who spent their lives in vain endeavors to subdue their natural affections, to repress, as offensive to God, every thought and feeling of sympathy with their fellow creatures.

If we desire to understand the determined cruelty of Satan, manifested for hundreds of years, not among those who never heard of God, but in the very heart and throughout the extent of Christendom, we have only to look at the history of Romanism. Through this mammoth system of deception the prince of evil achieves his purpose of bringing dishonor to God and wretchedness to man. And as we see how he succeeds in disguising himself and accomplishing his work through the leaders of the church, we may better understand why he has so great antipathy to the Bible. If that Book is read, the mercy and love of God will be revealed; it will be seen that He lays upon men none of these heavy burdens. All that He asks is a broken and contrite heart, a humble, obedient spirit.

Christ gives no example in His life for men and women to shut themselves in monasteries in order to become fitted for heaven. He has never taught that love and sympathy must be repressed. The Saviour's heart overflowed with love. The nearer man approaches to moral perfection, the keener are his sensibilities, the more acute is his perception of sin, and the deeper his sympathy for the afflicted. The pope claims to be the Vicar of Christ; but how does his character bear comparison with that of our Saviour? Was Christ ever known to consign men to the prison or the rack because they did not pay Him homage as the King of heaven? Was His voice heard condemning to death those who did not accept Him? When He was slighted by the people of a Samaritan village, the apostle John was filled with indignation, and inquired: "Lord, wilt Thou that we command fire to come down from heaven, and consume them, even as Elias did?" Jesus looked with pity upon His disciple, and rebuked his harsh spirit, saying: "The Son of man is not come to destroy men's lives, but to save them." Luke 9:54, 56. How different from the spirit manifested by Christ is that of His professed vicar.

The Roman Church now presents a fair front to the world, covering with apologies her record of horrible cruelties. She has clothed herself in Christlike garments; but she is unchanged. Every principle of the papacy that existed in past ages exists today. The doctrines devised in the darkest ages are still held. Let none deceive themselves. The papacy that Protestants are now so ready to honor is the same that ruled the world in the days of the Reformation, when men of God stood up, at the peril of their lives, to expose her iniquity. She possesses the same pride and arrogant assumption that lorded it over kings and princes, and claimed the prerogatives of God. Her spirit is no less cruel and despotic now than when she crushed out human liberty and slew the saints of the Most High.

The papacy is just what prophecy declared that she would be, the apostasy of the latter times (2 Thessalonians 2:3, 4). It is a part of her policy to assume the character which will best accomplish her purpose; but beneath the variable appearance of the chameleon she conceals the invariable venom of the serpent. "Faith ought not to be kept with heretics, nor persons suspected of heresy" (Lenfant, volume 1, page 516), she declares. Shall this power, whose record for a thousand years is written in the blood of the saints, be now acknowledged as a part of the church of Christ?

It is not without reason that the claim has been put forth in Protestant countries that Catholicism differs less widely from Protestantism than in former times. There has been a change; but the change is not in the papacy. Catholicism indeed resembles much of the Protestantism that now exists, because Protestantism has so greatly degenerated since the days of the Reformers.

As the Protestant churches have been seeking the favor of the world, false charity has blinded their eyes. They do not see but that it is right to believe good of all evil, and as the inevitable result they will finally believe evil of all good. Instead of standing in defense of the faith once delivered to the saints, they are now, as it were, apologizing to Rome for their uncharitable opinion of her, begging pardon for their bigotry.

A large class, even of those who look upon Romanism with no favor, apprehend little danger from her power and influence. Many urge that the intellectual and moral darkness prevailing during the Middle Ages favored the spread of her dogmas, superstitions, and oppression, and that the greater intelligence of modern times, the general diffusion of knowledge, and the increasing liberality in matters of religion forbid a revival of intolerance and tyranny. The very thought that such a state of things will exist in this enlightened age is ridiculed. It is true that great light, intellectual, moral, and religious, is shining upon this generation. In the open pages of God's Holy Word, light from heaven has been shed upon the world. But it should be remembered that the greater the light bestowed, the greater the darkness of those who pervert and reject it.

A prayerful study of the Bible would show Protestants the real character of the papacy and would cause them to abhor and to shun it; but many are so wise in their own conceit that they feel no need of humbly seeking God that they may be led into the truth. Although priding themselves on their enlightenment, they are ignorant both of the Scriptures and of the power of God. They must have some means of quieting their consciences, and they seek that which is least spiritual and humiliating. What they desire is a method of forgetting God which shall pass as a method of remembering Him. The papacy is well adapted to meet the wants of all these. It is prepared for two classes of mankind, embracing nearly the whole world—those who would be saved by their merits, and those who would be saved in their sins. Here is the secret of its power.

A day of great intellectual darkness has been shown to be favorable to the success of the papacy. It will yet be demonstrated that a day of great intellectual light is equally favorable for its success. In past ages, when men were without God's word and without the knowledge of the truth, their eyes were blindfolded, and thousands were ensnared, not seeing the net spread for their feet. In this generation there are many whose eyes become dazzled by the glare of human speculations, science falsely so called; they discern not the net, and walk into it as readily as if blindfolded. God designed that man's intellectual powers should be held as a gift from his Maker and should be employed in the service of truth and righteousness; but when pride and ambition are cherished, and men exalt their own theories above the word of God, then intelligence can accomplish greater harm than ignorance. Thus the false science of the present day, which undermines faith in the Bible, will prove as successful in preparing the way for the acceptance of the papacy, with its pleasing forms, as did the withholding of knowledge in opening the way for its aggrandizement in the Dark Ages.

In the movements now in progress in the United States to secure for the institutions and usages of the church the support of the state, Protestants are following in the steps of papists. Nay, more, they are opening the door for the papacy to regain in Protestant America the supremacy which she has lost in the Old World. And that which gives greater significance to this movement is the fact that the principal object contemplated is the enforcement of Sunday observance—a custom which originated with Rome, and which she claims as the sign of her authority. It is the spirit of the papacy—the spirit of conformity to worldly customs, the veneration for human traditions above the commandments of God—that is permeating the Protestant churches and leading them on to do the same work of Sunday exaltation which the Papacy has done before them.

If the reader would understand the agencies to be employed in the soon-coming contest, he has but to trace the record of the means which Rome employed for the same object in ages past. If he would know how papists and Protestants united will deal with those who reject their dogmas, let him see the spirit which Rome manifested toward the Sabbath and its defenders. Royal edicts, general councils, and church ordinances sustained by secular power were the steps by which the pagan festival attained its position of honor in the Christian world. The first public measure enforcing Sunday observance was the law enacted by Constantine (A.D. 321). This edict required townspeople to rest on "the venerable day of the sun," but permitted countrymen to continue their agricultural pursuits. Though virtually a heathen statute, it was enforced by the emperor after his nominal acceptance of Christianity.

The royal mandate not proving a sufficient substitute for divine authority, Eusebius, a bishop who sought the favor of princes, and who was the special friend and flatterer of Constantine, advanced the claim that Christ had transferred the Sabbath to Sunday. Not a single testimony of the Scriptures was produced in proof of the new doctrine. Eusebius himself unwittingly acknowledges its falsity and points to the real authors of the change. "All things", he says, "whatever that it was duty to do on the Sabbath, these we have transferred to the Lord's Day" (Robert Cox, Sabbath Laws and Sabbath Duties, page 538). But the Sunday argument, groundless as it was, served to embolden men in trampling upon the Sabbath of the Lord. All who desired to be honored by the world accepted the popular festival.

As the Papacy became firmly established, the work of Sunday exaltation was continued. For a time the people engaged in agricultural labor when not attending church, and the seventh day was still regarded as the Sabbath. But steadily a change was effected. Those in holy office were forbidden to pass judgment in any civil controversy on the Sunday. Soon after, all persons, of whatever rank, were commanded to refrain from common labor on pain of a fine for freemen and stripes in the case of servants. Later it was decreed that rich men should be punished with the loss of half of their estates; and finally, that if still obstinate they should be made slaves. The lower classes were to suffer perpetual banishment.

Miracles also were called into requisition. Among other wonders it was reported that as a husbandman who was about to plow his field on Sunday cleaned his plow with an iron, the iron stuck fast in his hand, and for two years he carried it about with him, to his exceeding great pain and shame (Francis West, Historical and Practical Discourse on the Lord's Day, page 174).

Later the pope gave directions that the parish priest should admonish the violators of Sunday and wishes them to go to church and say their prayers, lest they bring some great calamity on themselves and neighbors. An ecclesiastical council brought forward the argument, since so widely employed, even by Protestants, that because persons had been struck by lightning while laboring on Sunday, it must be the Sabbath. "It is apparent," said the prelates, "how high the displeasure of God was upon their neglect of this day." An appeal was then made that priests and ministers, kings and princes, and all faithful people use their utmost endeavors and care that the day be restored to its honor, and, for the credit of Christianity, more devoutly observed for the time to come" (Thomas Morer, Discourse in Six Dialogues on the Name, Notion, and Observation of the Lord's Day, page 271).

The decrees of councils proving insufficient, the secular authorities were besought to issue an edict that would strike terror to the hearts of the people and force them to refrain from labor on the Sunday. At a synod held in Rome, all previous decisions were reaffirmed with greater force and solemnity. They were also incorporated into the ecclesiastical law and enforced by the civil authorities throughout nearly all Christendom. (Heylyn, History of the Sabbath, pt. 2, ch. 5, sec. 7).

Still the absence of Scriptural authority for Sunday keeping occasioned no little embarrassment. The people questioned the right of their teachers to set aside the positive declaration of Jehovah, "The seventh day is the Sabbath of the Lord thy God," in order to honor the day of the sun. To supply the lack of Bible testimony, other expedients were necessary. A zealous advocate of Sunday, who about the close of the twelfth century visited the churches of England, was resisted by faithful witnesses for the truth; and so fruitless were his efforts that he departed from the country for a season and cast about him for some means to enforce his teachings. When he returned, the lack was supplied, and in his after labors he met with greater success. He brought with him a roll purporting to be from God Himself, which contained the needed command for Sunday observance, with awful threats to terrify the disobedient. This precious document— as base a counterfeit as the institution it supported—was said to have fallen from heaven and to have been found in Jerusalem, upon the altar of St. Simeon, in Golgotha. But, in fact, the pontifical palace at Rome was the source whence it proceeded. Frauds and forgeries to advance the power and prosperity of the church have in all ages been esteemed lawful by the papal hierarchy.

The roll forbade labor from the ninth hour, three o'clock, on Saturday afternoon, till sunrise on Monday; and its authority was declared to be confirmed by many miracles. It was reported that persons laboring beyond the appointed hour were stricken with paralysis. A miller who attempted to grind his corn, saw, instead of flour, a torrent of blood come forth, and the mill wheel stood still, notwithstanding the strong rush of water. A woman who placed dough in the oven found it raw when taken out, though the oven was very hot. Another who had dough prepared for baking at the ninth hour, but determined to set it aside till Monday, found, the next day, that it had been made into loaves and baked by divine power. A man who baked bread after the ninth hour on Saturday found, when he broke it the next morning that blood started there from. By such absurd and superstitious fabrications did the advocates of Sunday endeavor to establish its sacredness. (Roger de Hoveden, Annals, vol. 2, pp. 526-530.)

In Scotland, as in England, a greater regard for Sunday was secured by uniting with it a portion of the ancient Sabbath. But the time required to be kept holy varied. An edict from the king of Scotland declared that "Saturday from twelve at noon ought to be accounted holy," and that no man, from that time till Monday morning, should engage in worldly business" (Morer, pages 290, 291. But notwithstanding all the efforts to establish Sunday sacredness, papists themselves publicly confessed the divine authority of the Sabbath and the human origin of the institution by which it had been supplanted. In the sixteenth century a papal council plainly declared: "Let all Christians remember that the seventh day was consecrated by God, and hath been received and observed, not only by the Jews, but by all others who pretend to worship God; though we Christians have changed their Sabbath into the Lord's Day" (Ibid., pages 281, 282). Those who were tampering with the divine law were not ignorant of the character of their work. They were deliberately setting themselves above God.

A striking illustration of Rome's policy toward those who disagree with her was given in the long and bloody persecution of the Waldenses, some of whom were observers of the Sabbath. Others suffered in a similar manner for their fidelity to the fourth commandment. The history of the churches of Ethiopia and Abyssinia is especially significant. Amid the gloom of the Dark Ages, the Christians of Central Africa were lost sight of and forgotten by the world, and for many centuries they enjoyed freedom in the exercise of their faith. But at last Rome learned of their existence, and the emperor of Abyssinia was soon beguiled into an acknowledgment of the pope as the Vicar of Christ. Other concessions followed.

An edict was issued forbidding the observance of the Sabbath under the severest penalties. (Michael Geddes, Church History of Ethiopia, pages 311, 312.) But papal tyranny soon became a yoke so galling that the Abyssinians determined to break it from their necks. After a terrible struggle the Romanists were banished from their dominions, and the ancient faith was restored. The churches rejoiced in their freedom, and they never forgot the lesson they had learned concerning the deception, the fanaticism, and the despotic power of Rome. Within their solitary realm they were content to remain, unknown to the rest of Christendom.

The churches of Africa held the Sabbath as it was held by the papal church before her complete apostasy. While they kept the seventh day in obedience to the commandment of God, they abstained from labor on the Sunday in conformity to the custom of the church. Upon obtaining supreme power, Rome had trampled upon the Sabbath of God to exalt her own; but the churches of Africa, hidden for nearly a thousand years, did not share in this apostasy. When brought under the sway of Rome, they were forced to set aside the true and exalt the false sabbath; but no sooner had they regained their independence than they returned to obedience to the fourth commandment. These records of the past clearly reveal the enmity of Rome toward the true Sabbath and its defenders, and the means which she employs to honor the institution of her creating. The word of God teaches that these scenes are to be repeated as Roman Catholics and Protestants shall unite for the exaltation of the Sunday.

The prophecy of Revelation 13 declares that the power represented by the beast with lamblike horns shall cause "the earth and them which dwell therein" to worship the papacy —there symbolized by the beast "like unto a leopard." The beast with two horns is also to say "to them that dwell on the earth, that they should make an image to the beast"; and, furthermore, it is to command all, "both small and great, rich and poor, free and bond", to receive the mark of the beast. (Revelation 13:11-16). It has been shown that the United States is the power represented by the beast with lamblike horns, and that this prophecy will be fulfilled when the United States shall enforce Sunday observance, which Rome claims as the special acknowledgment of her supremacy. But in this homage to the papacy the United States will not be alone. The influence of Rome in the countries that once acknowledged her dominion is still far from being destroyed. And prophecy foretells a restoration of her power. "I saw one of his heads as it were wounded to death; and his deadly wound was healed: and all the world wondered after the beast" (Revelation 13:3:3). The infliction of the deadly wound points to the downfall of the papacy in 1798. After this, says the prophet, "his deadly wound was healed: and all the world wondered after the beast". Paul states plainly that the "man of sin" will continue until the second advent (2 Thessalonians 2:3-8). To the very close of time he will carry forward the work of deception. And the Revelator declares, also referring to the Papacy: "All that dwell upon the earth shall worship him, whose names are not written in the book of life" (Revelation 13:8). In both the Old and the New World, the Papacy will receive homage in the honor paid to the Sunday institution, that rests solely upon the authority of the Roman Church.

Since the middle of the nineteenth century, students of prophecy in the United States have presented this testimony to the world. In the events now taking place is seen a rapid advance toward the fulfillment of the prediction. With Protestant teachers there is the same claim of divine authority for Sunday keeping, and the same lack of Scriptural evidence, as with the papal leaders who fabricated miracles to supply the place of a command from God. The assertion that God's judgments are visited upon men for their violation of the Sunday-sabbath, will be repeated; already it is beginning to be urged. And a movement to enforce Sunday observance is fast gaining ground.

Marvelous in her shrewdness and cunning is the Roman Church. She can read what is to be. She bides her time, seeing that the Protestant churches are paying her homage in their acceptance of the false sabbath and that they are preparing to enforce it by the very means which she herself employed in bygone days. Those who reject the light of truth will yet seek the aid of this self-styled infallible power to exalt an institution that originated with her. How readily she will come to the help of Protestants in this work it is not difficult to conjecture. Who understands better than the papal leaders how to deal with those who are disobedient to the church?

The Roman Catholic Church, with all its ramifications throughout the world, forms one vast organization under the control, and designed to serve the interests, of the papal see. Its millions of communicants, in every country on the globe, are instructed to hold themselves as bound in allegiance to the pope. Whatever their nationality or their government, they are to regard the authority of the church as above all other. Though they may take the oath pledging their loyalty to the state, yet back of this lies the vow of obedience to Rome, absolving them from every pledge inimical to her interests.

History testifies of her artful and persistent efforts to insinuate herself into the affairs of nations; and having gained a foothold, to further her own aims, even at the ruin of princes and people. In the year 1204, Pope Innocent III extracted from Peter II, king of Arragon, the following extraordinary oath: "I, Peter, king of Arragonians, profess and promise to be ever faithful and obedient to my lord, Pope Innocent, to his Catholic successors, and the Roman Church, and faithfully to preserve my kingdom in his obedience, defending the Catholic faith, and persecuting heretical pravity". (John Dowling, The History of Romanism, b. 5, ch. 6, sec. 55). This is in harmony with the claims regarding the power of the Roman pontiff that it is lawful for him to depose emperors and that he can absolve subjects from their allegiance to unrighteous rulers (Mosheim, b. 3, cent. 11, pt. 2, ch. 2, sec. 9, note 17).

And let it be remembered, it is the boast of Rome that she never changes. The principles of Gregory VII and Innocent III are still the principles of the Roman Catholic Church. And had she but the power, she would put them in practice with as much vigor now as in past centuries. Protestants little know what they are doing when they propose to accept the aid of Rome in the work of Sunday exaltation. While they are bent upon the accomplishment of their purpose, Rome is aiming to re-establish her power, to recover her lost supremacy. Let the principle once be established in the United States that the church may employ or control the power of the state; that religious observances may be enforced by secular laws; in short, that the authority of church and state is to dominate the conscience and the triumph of Rome in this country is assured.

God's word has given warning of the impending danger; let this be unheeded, and the Protestant world will learn what the purposes of Rome really are, only when it is too late to escape the snare. She is silently growing into power. Her doctrines are exerting their influence in legislative halls, in the churches, and in the hearts of men. She is piling up her lofty and massive structures in the secret recesses of which her former persecutions will be repeated. Stealthily and unsuspectedly she is strengthening her forces to further her own ends when the time shall come for her to strike. All that she desires is vantage ground, and this is already being given her. We shall soon see and shall feel what the purpose of the Roman element is. Whoever shall believe and obey the word of God will thereby incur reproach and persecution.

CHAPTER 9

The Impending Conflict

From the very beginning of the great controversy in heaven it has been Satan's purpose to overthrow the law of God. It was to accomplish this that he entered upon his rebellion against the Creator, and though he was cast out of heaven he has continued the same warfare upon the earth. To deceive men, and thus lead them to transgress God's law, is the object which he has steadfastly pursued. Whether this be accomplished by casting aside the law altogether, or by rejecting one of its precepts, the result will be ultimately the same. He that offends "in one point", manifests contempt for the whole law; his influence and example are on the side of transgression; he becomes "guilty of all" (James 2:10).

In seeking to cast contempt upon the divine statutes, Satan has perverted the doctrines of the Bible, and errors have thus become incorporated into the faith of thousands who profess to believe the Scriptures. The last great conflict between truth and error is but the final struggle of the long-standing controversy concerning the law of God. Upon this battle we are now entering—a battle between the laws of men and the precepts of Jehovah, between the religion of the Bible and the religion of fable and tradition.

The agencies which will unite against truth and righteousness in this contest are now actively at work. God's holy word, which has been handed down to us at such a cost of suffering and blood, is but little valued. The Bible is within the reach of all, but there are few who really accept it as the guide of life. Infidelity prevails to an alarming extent, not in the world merely, but in the church. Many have come to deny doctrines which are the very pillars of the Christian faith. The great facts of creation as presented by the inspired writers, the fall of man, the atonement, and the perpetuity of the law of God, are practically rejected, either wholly or in part, by a large share of the professedly Christian world. Thousands who pride themselves upon their wisdom and independence regard it as an evidence of weakness to place implicit confidence in the Bible; they think it a proof of superior talent and learning to cavil at the Scriptures and to spiritualize and explain away their most important truths. Many ministers are teaching their people, and many professors and teachers are instructing their students, that the law of God has been changed or abrogated; and those who regard its requirements as still valid, to be literally obeyed, are thought to be deserving only of ridicule or contempt.

In rejecting the truth, men reject its Author. In trampling upon the law of God, they deny the authority of the Law-giver. It is as easy to make an idol of false doctrines and theories as to fashion an idol of wood or stone. By misrepresenting the attributes of God, Satan leads men to conceive of Him in a false character. With many, a philosophical idol is enthroned in the place of Jehovah; while the living God, as He is revealed in His word, in Christ, and in the works of creation, is worshiped by but few. Thousands deify nature while they deny the God of nature. Though in a different form, idolatry exists in the Christian world today as verily as it existed among ancient Israel in the days of Elijah. The god of many professedly wise men, of philosophers, poets, politicians, journalists—the god of polished fashionable circles, of many colleges and universities, even of some theological institutions—is little better than Baal, the sun-god of Phoenicia.

No error accepted by the Christian world strikes more boldly against the authority of Heaven, none is more directly opposed to the dictates of reason; none is more pernicious in its results, than the modern doctrine, so rapidly gaining ground that God's law is no longer binding upon men. Every nation has its laws, which command respect and obedience; no government could exist without them; and can it be conceived that the Creator of the heavens and the earth has no law to govern the beings He has made? Suppose that prominent ministers were publicly to teach that the statutes which govern their land and protect the rights of its citizens were not obligatory—that they restricted the liberties of the people, and therefore ought not to be obeyed; how long would such men be tolerated in the pulpit? But is it a graver offense to disregard the laws of states and nations than to trample upon those divine precepts which are the foundation of all government?

It would be far more consistent for nations to abolish their statutes, and permit the people to do as they please, than for the Ruler of the universe to annul His law, and leave the world without a standard to condemn the guilty or justify the obedient. Would we know the result of making void the law of God? The experiment has been tried. Terrible were the scenes enacted in France when atheism became the controlling power. It was then demonstrated to the world that to throw off the restraints which God has imposed is to accept the rule of the cruelest of tyrants. When the standard of righteousness is set aside, the way is open for the prince of evil to establish his power in the earth.

Wherever the divine precepts are rejected, sin ceases to appear sinful or righteousness desirable. Those who refuse to submit to the government of God are wholly unfitted to govern themselves. Through their pernicious teachings the spirit of insubordination is implanted in the hearts of children and youth, who are naturally impatient of control; and a lawless, licentious state of society results. While scoffing at the credulity of those who obey the requirements of God, the multitudes eagerly accept the delusions of Satan. They give the rein to lust and practice the sins which have called down judgments upon the heathen.

Those who teach the people to regard lightly the commandments of God sow disobedience to reap disobedience. Let the restraint imposed by the divine law be wholly cast aside, and human laws would soon be disregarded. Because God forbids dishonest practices, coveting, lying, and defrauding, men are ready to trample upon His statutes as a hindrance to their worldly prosperity; but the results of banishing these precepts would be such as they do not anticipate. If the law were not binding, why should any fear to transgress? Property would no longer be safe. Men would obtain their neighbor's possessions by violence, and the strongest would become richest. Life itself would not be respected. The marriage vow would no longer stand as a sacred bulwark to protect the family. He who had the power, would, if he desired, take his neighbor's wife by violence. The fifth commandment would be set aside with the fourth. Children would not shrink from taking the life of their parents if by so doing they could obtain the desire of their corrupt hearts. The civilized world would become a horde of robbers and assassins; and peace, rest, and happiness would be banished from the earth.

Already the doctrine that men are released from obedience to God's requirements has weakened the force of moral obligation and opened the floodgates of iniquity upon the world. Lawlessness, dissipation, and corruption are sweeping in upon us like an overwhelming tide. In the family, Satan is at work. His banner waves, even in professedly Christian households. There is envy, evil surmising, hypocrisy, estrangement, emulation, strife, betrayal of sacred trusts, indulgence of lust. The whole system of religious principles and doctrines, which should form the foundation and framework of social life, seems to be a tottering mass, ready to fall to ruin. The vilest of criminals, when thrown into prison for their offenses, are often made the recipients of gifts and attentions as if they had attained an enviable distinction. Great publicity is given to their character and crimes. The press publishes the revolting details of vice, thus initiating others into the practice of fraud, robbery, and murder; and Satan exults in the success of his hellish schemes. The infatuation of vice, the wanton taking of life, the terrible increase of intemperance and iniquity of every order and degree, should arouse all who fear God, to inquire what can be done to stay the tide of evil.

Courts of justice are corrupt. Rulers are actuated by desire for gain and love of sensual pleasure. Intemperance has beclouded the faculties of many so that Satan has almost complete control of them. Jurists are perverted, bribed, deluded. Drunkenness and revelry, passion, envy, dishonesty of every sort, are represented among those who administer the laws. "Justice standeth afar off: for truth is fallen in the street, and equity cannot enter" (Isaiah 59:14).

The iniquity and spiritual darkness that prevailed under the supremacy of Rome were the inevitable result of her suppression of the Scriptures; but where is to be found the cause of the widespread infidelity, the rejection of the law of God, and the consequent corruption, under the full blaze of gospel light in an age of religious freedom? Now that Satan can no longer keep the world under his control by withholding the Scriptures, he resorts to other means to accomplish the same object. To destroy faith in the Bible serves his purpose as well as to destroy the Bible itself. By introducing the belief that God's law is not binding, he as effectually leads men to transgress as if they were wholly ignorant of its precepts. And now, as in former ages, he has worked through the church to further his designs.

The religious organizations of the day have refused to listen to unpopular truths plainly brought to view in the Scriptures, and in combating them they have adopted interpretations and taken positions which have sown broadcast the seeds of skepticism. Clinging to the papal error of natural immortality and man's consciousness in death, they have rejected the only defense against the delusions of spiritualism. The doctrine of eternal torment has led many to disbelieve the Bible. And as the claims of the fourth commandment are urged upon the people, it is found that the observance of the seventh-day Sabbath is enjoined; and as the only way to free themselves from a duty which they are unwilling to perform, many popular teachers declare that the law of God is no longer binding. Thus they cast away the law and the Sabbath together.

As the work of Sabbath reform extends, this rejection of the divine law to avoid the claims of the fourth commandment will become well-nigh universal. The teachings of religious leaders have opened the door to infidelity, to spiritualism, and to contempt for God's holy law; and upon these leaders rests a fearful responsibility for the iniquity that exists in the Christian world.

Yet this very class put forth the claim that the fast-spreading corruption is largely attributable to the desecration of the so-called "Christian Sabbath", and that the enforcement of Sunday observance would greatly improve the morals of society. This claim is especially urged in America, where the doctrine of the true Sabbath has been most widely preached. Here the temperance work, one of the most prominent and important of moral reforms, is often combined with the Sunday movement, and the advocates of the latter represent themselves as laboring to promote the highest interest of society; and those who refuse to unite with them are denounced as the enemies of temperance and reform.

But the fact that a movement to establish error is connected with a work which is in itself good, is not an argument in favor of the error. We may disguise poison by mingling it with wholesome food, but we do not change its nature. On the contrary, it is rendered more dangerous, as it is more likely to be taken unawares. It is one of Satan's devices to combine with falsehood just enough truth to give it plausibility. The leaders of the Sunday movement may advocate reforms which the people need, principles which are in harmony with the Bible; yet while there is with these a requirement which is contrary to God's law, His servants cannot unite with them. Nothing can justify them in setting aside the commandments of God for the precepts of men.

Through the two great errors, the immortality of the soul and Sunday sacredness, Satan will bring the people under his deceptions. While the former lays the foundation of spiritualism, the latter creates a bond of sympathy with Rome. The Protestants of the United States will be foremost in stretching their hands across the gulf to grasp the hand of spiritualism; they will reach over the abyss to clasp hands with the Roman power; and under the influence of this threefold union, this country will follow in the steps of Rome in trampling on the rights of conscience. As spiritualism more closely imitates the nominal Christianity of the day, it has greater power to deceive and ensnare. Satan himself is converted, after the modern order of things. He will appear in the character of an angel of light. Through the agency of spiritualism, miracles will be wrought, the sick will be healed, and many undeniable wonders will be performed. And as the spirits will profess faith in the Bible, and manifest respect for the institutions of the church, their work will be accepted as a manifestation of divine power.

The line of distinction between professed Christians and the ungodly is now hardly distinguishable. Church members love what the world loves and are ready to join with them, and Satan determines to unite them in one body and thus strengthen his cause by sweeping all into the ranks of spiritualism. Papists, who boast of miracles as a certain sign of the true church, will be readily deceived by this wonder-working power; and Protestants, having cast away the shield of truth, will also be deluded. Papists, Protestants, and worldlings will alike accept the form of godliness without the power, and they will see in this union a grand movement for the conversion of the world and the ushering in of the long-expected millennium.

Through spiritualism, Satan appears as a benefactor of the race, healing the diseases of the people, and professing to present a new and more exalted system of religious faith; but at the same time he works as a destroyer. His temptations are leading multitudes to ruin. Intemperance dethrones reason; sensual indulgence, strife, and bloodshed follow. Satan delights in war, for it excites the worst passions of the soul and then sweeps into eternity its victims steeped in vice and blood. It is his object to incite the nations to war against one another, for he can thus divert the minds of the people from the work of preparation to stand in the day of God.

Satan works through the elements also to garner his harvest of unprepared souls. He has studied the secrets of the laboratories of nature, and he uses all his power to control the elements as far as God allows. When he was suffered to afflict Job, how quickly flocks and herds, servants, houses, children, were swept away, one trouble succeeding another as in a moment. It is God that shields His creatures and hedges them in from the power of the destroyer. But the Christian world have shown contempt for the law of Jehovah; and the Lord will do just what He has declared that He would—He will withdraw His blessings from the earth and remove His protecting care from those who are rebelling against His law and teaching and forcing others to do the same. Satan has control of all whom God does not especially guard. He will favor and prosper some in order to further his own designs, and he will bring trouble upon others and lead men to believe that it is God who is afflicting them.

While appearing to the children of men as a great physician who can heal all their maladies, he will bring disease and disaster, until populous cities are reduced to ruin and desolation. Even now he is at work. In accidents and calamities by sea and by land, in great conflagrations, in fierce tornadoes and terrific hailstorms, in tempests, floods, cyclones, tidal waves, and earthquakes, in every place and in a thousand forms, Satan is exercising his power. He sweeps away the ripening harvest, and famine and distress follow. He imparts to the air a deadly taint, and thousands perish by the pestilence. These visitations are to become more and more frequent and disastrous. Destruction will be upon both man and beast. "The earth mourneth and fadeth away, the haughty people do languish. The earth also is defiled under the inhabitants thereof; because they have transgressed the laws, changed the ordinance, broken the everlasting covenant" (Isaiah 24:4, 5).

And then the great deceiver will persuade men that those who serve God are causing these evils. The class that has provoked the displeasure of Heaven will charge all their troubles upon those whose obedience to God's commandments is a perpetual reproof to transgressors. It will be declared that men are offending God by the violation of the Sunday sabbath; that this sin has brought calamities which will not cease until Sunday observance shall be strictly enforced; and that those who present the claims of the fourth commandment, thus destroying reverence for Sunday, are troublers of the people, preventing their restoration to divine favor and temporal prosperity. Thus the accusation urged of old against the servant of God will be repeated and upon grounds equally well established: "And it came to pass, when Ahab saw Elijah, that Ahab said unto him, Art thou he that troubleth Israel? And he answered, I have not troubled Israel; but thou, and thy father's house, in that ye have forsaken the commandments of the Lord, and thou hast followed Baalim" (1 Kings 18:17, 18). As the wrath of the people shall be excited by false charges, they will pursue a course toward God's ambassadors very similar to that which apostate Israel pursued toward Elijah.

The miracle-working power manifested through spiritualism will exert its influence against those who choose to obey God rather than men. Communications from the spirits will declare that God has sent them to convince the rejecters of Sunday of their error, affirming that the laws of the land should be obeyed as the law of God. They will lament the great wickedness in the world and second the testimony of religious teachers that the degraded state of morals is caused by the desecration of Sunday. Great will be the indignation excited against all who refuse to accept their testimony.

Satan's policy in this final conflict with God's people is the same that he employed in the opening of the great controversy in heaven. He professed to be seeking to promote the stability of the divine government, while secretly bending every effort to secure its overthrow. And the very work which he was thus endeavoring to accomplish he charged upon the loyal angels. The same policy of deception has marked the history of the Roman Church. It has professed to act as the vicegerent of Heaven, while seeking to exalt itself above God and to change His law. Under the rule of Rome, those who suffered death for their fidelity to the gospel were denounced as evildoers; they were declared to be in league with Satan; and every possible means was employed to cover them with reproach, to cause them to appear in the eyes of the people and even to themselves as the vilest of criminals. So it will be now. While Satan seeks to destroy those who honor God's law, he will cause them to be accused as lawbreakers, as men who are dishonoring God and bringing judgments upon the world.

God never forces the will or the conscience; but Satan's constant resort—to gain control of those whom he cannot otherwise seduce—is compulsion by cruelty. Through fear or force he endeavors to rule the conscience and to secure homage to himself. To accomplish this, he works through both religious and secular authorities, moving them to the enforcement of human laws in defiance of the law of God.

Those who honor the Bible Sabbath will be denounced as enemies of law and order, as breaking down the moral restraints of society, causing anarchy and corruption, and calling down the judgments of God upon the earth. Their conscientious scruples will be pronounced obstinacy, stubbornness, and contempt of authority. They will be accused of disaffection toward the government. Ministers who deny the obligation of the divine law will present from the pulpit the duty of yielding obedience to the civil authorities as ordained of God. In legislative halls and courts of justice, commandment keepers will be misrepresented and condemned. A false coloring will be given to their words; the worst construction will be put upon their motives.

As the Protestant churches reject the clear, Scriptural arguments in defense of God's law, they will long to silence those whose faith they cannot overthrow by the Bible. Though they blind their own eyes to the fact, they are now adopting a course which will lead to the persecution of those who conscientiously refuse to do what the rest of the Christian world are doing, and acknowledge the claims of the Papal sabbath.

The dignitaries of church and state will unite to bribe, persuade, or compel all classes to honor the Sunday. The lack of divine authority will be supplied by oppressive enactments. Political corruption is destroying love of justice and regard for truth; and even in free America, rulers and legislators, in order to secure public favor, will yield to the popular demand for a law enforcing Sunday observance. Liberty of conscience, which has cost so great a sacrifice, will no longer be respected. In the soon-coming conflict we shall see exemplified the prophet's words: "The dragon was wroth with the woman, and went to make war with the remnant of her seed, which keep the commandments of God, and have the testimony of Jesus Christ" (Revelation 12:17).

CHAPTER 10

The Scriptures our Only Safeguard

"To the law and to the testimony: if they speak not according to this word, it is because there is no light in them" (Isaiah 8:20). The people of God are directed to the Scriptures as their safeguard against the influence of false teachers and the delusive power of spirits of darkness. Satan employs every possible device to prevent men from obtaining a knowledge of the Bible; for its plain utterances reveal his deceptions. At every revival of God's work the prince of evil is aroused to more intense activity; he is now putting forth his utmost efforts for a final struggle against Christ and His followers. The last great delusion is soon to open before us. Antichrist is to perform his marvelous works in our sight. So closely will the counterfeit resemble the true that it will be impossible to distinguish between them except by the Holy Scriptures. By their testimony every statement and every miracle must be tested.

Those who endeavor to obey all the commandments of God will be opposed and derided. They can stand only in God. In order to endure the trial before them, they must understand the will of God as revealed in His word; they can honor Him only as they have a right conception of His character, government, and purposes, and act in accordance with them. None but those who have fortified the mind with the truths of the Bible will stand through the last great conflict. To every soul will come the searching test: Shall I obey God rather than men? The decisive hour is even now at hand. Are our feet planted on the rock of God's immutable word? Are we prepared to stand firm in defense of the commandments of God and the faith of Jesus?

Before His crucifixion the Saviour explained to His disciples that He was to be put to death and to rise again from the tomb, and angels were present to impress His words on minds and hearts. But the disciples were looking for temporal deliverance from the Roman yoke, and they could not tolerate the thought that He in whom all their hopes centered should suffer an ignominious death. The words which they needed to remember were banished from their minds; and when the time of trial came, it found them unprepared. The death of Jesus as fully destroyed their hopes as if He had not forewarned them. So in the prophecies the future is opened before us as plainly as it was opened to the disciples by the words of Christ. The events connected with the close of probation and the work of preparation for the time of trouble, are clearly presented. But multitudes have no more understanding of these important truths than if they had never been revealed. Satan watches to catch away every impression that would make them wise unto salvation, and the time of trouble will find them unready.

When God sends to men warnings so important that they are represented as proclaimed by holy angels flying in the midst of heaven, He requires every person endowed with reasoning powers to heed the message. The fearful judgments denounced against the worship of the beast and his image (Revelation 14:9-11), should lead all to a diligent study of the prophecies to learn what the mark of the beast is, and how they are to avoid receiving it. But the masses of the people turn away their ears from hearing the truth and are turned unto fables. The apostle Paul declared, looking down to the last days: "The time will come when they will not endure sound doctrine." 2 Timothy 4:3. That time has fully come. The multitudes do not want Bible truth, because it interferes with the desires of the sinful, world-loving heart; and Satan supplies the deceptions which they love.

But God will have a people upon the earth to maintain the Bible, and the Bible only, as the standard of all doctrines and the basis of all reforms. The opinions of learned men, the deductions of science, the creeds or decisions of ecclesiastical councils, as numerous and discordant as are the churches which they represent, the voice of the majority—not one nor all of these should be regarded as evidence for or against any point of religious faith. Before accepting any doctrine or precept, we should demand a plain "Thus saith the Lord" in its support.

Satan is constantly endeavoring to attract attention to man in the place of God. He leads the people to look to bishops, to pastors, to professors of theology, as their guides, instead of searching the Scriptures to learn their duty for themselves. Then, by controlling the minds of these leaders, he can influence the multitudes according to his will.

When Christ came to speak the words of life, the common people heard Him gladly; and many, even of the priests and rulers, believed on Him. But the chief of the priesthood and the leading men of the nation were determined to condemn and repudiate His teachings. Though they were baffled in all their efforts to find accusations against Him, though they could not but feel the influence of the divine power and wisdom attending His words, yet they incased themselves in prejudice; they rejected the clearest evidence of His Messiahship, lest they should be forced to become His disciples. These opponents of Jesus were men whom the people had been taught from infancy to reverence, to whose authority they had been accustomed implicitly to bow. "How is it," they asked, "that our rulers and learned scribes do not believe on Jesus? Would not these pious men receive Him if He were the Christ?" It was the influence of such teachers that led the Jewish nation to reject their Redeemer.

The spirit which actuated those priests and rulers is still manifested by many who make a high profession of piety. They refuse to examine the testimony of the Scriptures concerning the special truths for this time. They point to their own numbers, wealth, and popularity, and look with contempt upon the advocates of truth as few, poor, and unpopular, having a faith that separates them from the world.

Christ foresaw that the undue assumption of authority indulged by the scribes and Pharisees would not cease with the dispersion of the Jews. He had a prophetic view of the work of exalting human authority to rule the conscience, which has been so terrible a curse to the church in all ages. And His fearful denunciations of the scribes and Pharisees, and His warnings to the people not to follow these blind leaders, were placed on record as an admonition to future generations.

The Roman Church reserves to the clergy the right to interpret the Scriptures. On the ground that ecclesiastics alone are competent to explain God's word, it is withheld from the common people. Though the Reformation gave the Scriptures to all, yet the selfsame principle which was maintained by Rome prevents multitudes in Protestant churches from searching the Bible for themselves. They are taught to accept its teachings as interpreted by the church; and there are thousands who dare receive nothing, however plainly revealed in Scripture, that is contrary to their creed or the established teaching of their church.

Notwithstanding the Bible is full of warnings against false teachers, many are ready thus to commit the keeping of their souls to the clergy. There are today thousands of professors of religion who can give no other reason for points of faith which they hold than that they were so instructed by their religious leaders. They pass by the Saviour's teachings almost unnoticed, and place implicit confidence in the words of the ministers. But are ministers infallible? How can we trust our souls to their guidance unless we know from God's word that they are light bearers? A lack of moral courage to step aside from the beaten track of the world leads many to follow in the steps of learned men; and by their reluctance to investigate for themselves, they are becoming hopelessly fastened in the chains of error.

They see that the truth for this time is plainly brought to view in the Bible; and they feel the power of the Holy Spirit attending its proclamation; yet they allow the opposition of the clergy to turn them from the light. Though reason and conscience are convinced, these deluded souls dare not think differently from the minister; and their individual judgment, their eternal interests, are sacrificed to the unbelief, the pride and prejudice, of another.

Many are the ways by which Satan works through human influence to bind his captives. He secures multitudes to himself by attaching them by the silken cords of affection to those who are enemies of the cross of Christ. Whatever this attachment may be, parental, filial, conjugal, or social, the effect is the same; the opposers of truth exert their power to control the conscience, and the souls held under their sway have not sufficient courage or independence to obey their own convictions of duty.

The truth and the glory of God are inseparable; it is impossible for us, with the Bible within our reach, to honor God by erroneous opinions. Many claim that it matters not what one believes, if his life is only right. But the life is molded by the faith. If light and truth is within our reach, and we neglect to improve the privilege of hearing and seeing it, we virtually reject it; we are choosing darkness rather than light.

"There is a way that seemeth right unto a man, but the end thereof are the ways of death" (Proverbs 16:25). Ignorance is no excuse for error or sin, when there is every opportunity to know the will of God. A man is traveling and comes to a place where there are several roads and a guideboard indicating where each one leads. If he disregards the guideboard, and takes whichever road seems to him to be right, he may be ever so sincere, but will in all probability find himself on the wrong road.

God has given us His word that we may become acquainted with its teachings and know for ourselves what He requires of us. When the lawyer came to Jesus with the inquiry, "What shall I do to inherit eternal life?" the Saviour referred him to the Scriptures, saying: "What is written in the law? How readest thou?" (Matthew 19:17). Ignorance will not excuse young or old, nor release them from the punishment due for the transgression of God's law; because there is in their hands a faithful presentation of that law and of its principles and claims. It is not enough to have good intentions; it is not enough to do what a man thinks is right or what the minister tells him is right. His soul's salvation is at stake, and he should search the Scriptures for himself. However strong may be his convictions, however confident he may be that the minister knows what is truth, this is not his foundation. He has a chart pointing out every way mark on the heavenward journey, and he ought not to guess at anything.

It is the first and highest duty of every rational being to learn from the Scriptures what is truth, and then to walk in the light and encourage others to follow his example. We should day by day study the Bible diligently, weighing every thought and comparing scripture with scripture. With divine help we are to form our opinions for ourselves as we are to answer for ourselves before God.

The truths most plainly revealed in the Bible have been involved in doubt and darkness by learned men, who, with a pretense of great wisdom, teach that the Scriptures have a mystical, a secret, spiritual meaning not apparent in the language employed. These men are false teachers. It was to such a class that Jesus declared: "Ye know not the Scriptures, neither the power of God." Mark 12:24. The language of the Bible should be explained according to its obvious meaning, unless a symbol or figure is employed. Christ has given the promise: "If any man will do His will, he shall know of the doctrine." John 7:17. If men would but take the Bible as it reads, if there were no false teachers to mislead and confuse their minds, a work would be accomplished that would make angels glad and that would bring into the fold of Christ thousands upon thousands who are now wandering in error.

We should exert all the powers of the mind in the study of the Scriptures and should task the understanding to comprehend, as far as mortals can, the deep things of God; yet we must not forget that the docility and submission of a child is the true spirit of the learner. Scriptural difficulties can never be mastered by the same methods that are employed in grappling with philosophical problems. We should not engage in the study of the Bible with that self-reliance with which so many enter the domains of science, but with a prayerful dependence upon God and a sincere desire to learn His will. We must come with a humble and teachable spirit to obtain knowledge from the great I AM. Otherwise, evil angels will so blind our minds and harden our hearts that we shall not be impressed by the truth.

Many a portion of Scripture which learned men pronounce a mystery, or pass over as unimportant, is full of comfort and instruction to him who has been taught in the school of Christ. One reason why many theologians have no clearer understanding of God's word is, they close their eyes to truths which they do not wish to practice. As understanding of Bible truth depends not so much on the power of intellect brought to the search as on the singleness of purpose, the earnest longing after righteousness.

The Bible should never be studied without prayer. The Holy Spirit alone can cause us to feel the importance of those things easy to be understood, or prevent us from wresting truths difficult of comprehension. It is the office of heavenly angels to prepare the heart so to comprehend God's word that we shall be charmed with its beauty, admonished by its warnings, or animated and strengthened by its promises. We should make the psalmist's petition our own: "Open Thou mine eyes, that I may behold wondrous things out of Thy law" (Psalm 119:18). Temptations often appear irresistible because, through neglect of prayer and the study of the Bible, the tempted one cannot readily remember God's promises and meet Satan with the Scripture weapons. But angels are round about those who are willing to be taught in divine things; and in the time of great necessity they will bring to their remembrance the very truths which are needed. "Thus when the enemy shall come in like a flood, the Spirit of the Lord shall lift up a standard against him" (Isaiah 59:19).

Jesus promised His disciples: "The Comforter, which is the Holy Ghost, whom the Father will send in My name, He shall teach you all things, and bring all things to your remembrance, whatsoever I have said unto you" (John 14:26). But the teachings of Christ must previously have been stored in the mind in order for the Spirit of God to bring them to our remembrance in the time of peril. "Thy word have I hid in mine heart" said David, "that I might not sin against Thee" (Psalm 119:11).

All who value their eternal interests should be on their guard against the inroads of skepticism. The very pillars of truth will be assailed. It is impossible to keep beyond the reach of the sarcasms and sophisms, the insidious and pestilent teachings, of modern infidelity. Satan adapts his temptations to all classes. He assails the illiterate with a jest or sneer, while he meets the educated with scientific objections and philosophical reasoning, alike calculated to excite distrust or contempt of the Scriptures. Even youth of little experience presume to insinuate doubts concerning the fundamental principles of Christianity. And this youthful infidelity, shallow as it is, has its influence. Many are thus led to jest at the faith of their fathers and to do despite to the Spirit of grace (Hebrews 10:29). Many a life that promised to be an honor to God and a blessing to the world has been blighted by the foul breath of infidelity. All who trust to the boastful decisions of human reason and imagine that they can explain divine mysteries and arrive at truth unaided by the wisdom of God are entangled in the snare of Satan.

We are living in the most solemn period of this world's history. The destiny of earth's teeming multitudes is about to be decided. Our own future well-being and also the salvation of other souls depend upon the course which we now pursue. We need to be guided by the Spirit of truth. Every follower of Christ should earnestly inquire: "Lord, what wilt Thou have me to do?" We need to humble ourselves before the Lord, with fasting and prayer, and to meditate much upon His word, especially upon the scenes of the judgment. We should now seek a deep and living experience in the things of God. We have not a moment to lose. Events of vital importance are taking place around us; we are on Satan's enchanted ground. Sleep not, sentinels of God; the foe is lurking near, ready at any moment, should you become lax and drowsy, to spring upon you and make you his prey.

Many are deceived as to their true condition before God. They congratulate themselves upon the wrong acts which they do not commit, and forget to enumerate the good and noble deeds which God requires of them, but which they have neglected to perform. It is not enough that they are trees in the garden of God. They are to answer His expectation by bearing fruit. He holds them accountable for their failure to accomplish all the good which they could have done, through His grace strengthening them. In the books of heaven they are registered as cumberers of the ground. Yet the case of even this class is not utterly hopeless. With those who have slighted God's mercy and abused His grace, the heart of long-suffering love yet pleads: "Wherefore He saith, Awake thou that sleepest, and arise from the dead, and Christ shall give thee light. See then that ye walk circumspectly not as fools, but as wise. Redeeming the time, because the days are evil" (Ephesians 5:14-16).

When the testing time shall come, those who have made God's word their rule of life will be revealed. In summer there is no noticeable difference between evergreens and other trees; but when the blasts of winter come, the evergreens remain unchanged, while other trees are stripped of their foliage. So the falsehearted professor may not now be distinguished from the real Christian, but the time is just upon us when the difference will be apparent. Let opposition arise, let bigotry and intolerance again bear sway, let persecution be kindled, and the halfhearted and hypocritical will waver and yield the faith; but the true Christian will stand firm as a rock, his faith stronger, his hope brighter, than in days of prosperity.

Says the psalmist: "Thy testimonies are my meditation…Through Thy precepts I get understanding: therefore I hate every false way" (Psalm 119:99, 104). "Happy is the man that findeth wisdom…He shall be as a tree planted by the waters, and that spreadeth out her roots by the river, and shall not see when heat cometh, but her leaf shall be green; and shall not be careful in the year of drought, neither shall cease from yielding fruit" (Proverbs 3:13; Jeremiah 17:8).

CHAPTER 11

The Final Warning

"*I* saw another angel come down from heaven, having great power; and the earth was lightened with his glory. And he cried mightily with a strong voice, saying, Babylon the great is fallen, is fallen, and is become the habitation of devils, and the hold of every foul spirit, and a cage of every unclean and hateful bird…And I heard another voice from heaven, saying, Come out of her, My people, that ye be not partakers of her sins, and that ye receive not of her plagues" (Revelation 18:1, 2, 4). This scripture points forward to a time when the announcement of the fall of Babylon, as made by the second angel of Revelation 14 verse 8, is to be repeated, with the additional mention of the corruptions which have been entering the various organizations that constitute Babylon, since that message was first given, in the summer of 1844. A terrible condition of the religious world is here described.

With every rejection of truth the minds of the people will become darker, their hearts more stubborn, until they are entrenched in an infidel hardihood. In defiance of the warnings which God has given, they will continue to trample upon one of the precepts of the Decalogue, until they are led to persecute those who hold it sacred. Christ is set at nought in the contempt placed upon His word and His people. As the teachings of spiritualism are accepted by the churches, the restraint imposed upon the carnal heart is removed, and the profession of religion will become a cloak to conceal the basest iniquity. A belief in spiritual manifestations opens the door to seducing spirits and doctrines of devils, and thus the influence of evil angels will be felt in the churches.

Of Babylon, at the time brought to view in this prophecy, it is declared: "Her sins have reached unto heaven, and God hath remembered her iniquities" (Revelation 18:5). She has filled up the measure of her guilt, and destruction is about to fall upon her. But God still has a people in Babylon; and before the visitation of His judgments these faithful ones must be called out, that they partake not of her sins and "receive not of her plagues." Hence the movement symbolized by the angel coming down from heaven, lightening the earth with his glory and crying mightily with a strong voice, announcing the sins of Babylon. In connection with his message the call is heard: "Come out of her, My people". These announcements, uniting with the third angel's message, constitute the final warning to be given to the inhabitants of the earth.

Fearful is the issue to which the world is to be brought. The powers of earth, uniting to war against the commandments of God, will decree that "all, both small and great, rich and poor, free and bond" (Revelation 13:16), shall conform to the customs of the church by the observance of the false sabbath. All who refuse compliance will be visited with civil penalties, and it will finally be declared that they are deserving of death. On the other hand, the law of God enjoining the Creator's rest day demands obedience and threatens wrath against all who transgress its precepts.

With the issue thus clearly brought before him, whoever shall trample upon God's law to obey a human enactment receives the mark of the beast; he accepts the sign of allegiance to the power which he chooses to obey instead of God. The warning from heaven is: "If any man worship the beast and his image, and receive his mark in his forehead, or in his hand, the same shall drink of the wine of the wrath of God, which is poured out without mixture into the cup of His indignation" (Revelation 14:9, 10).

But not one is made to suffer the wrath of God until the truth has been brought home to his mind and conscience, and has been rejected. There are many who have never had an opportunity to hear the special truths for this time. The obligation of the fourth commandment has never been set before them in its true light. He who reads every heart and tries every motive will leave none who desire a knowledge of the truth, to be deceived as to the issues of the controversy. The decree is not to be urged upon the people blindly. Everyone is to have sufficient light to make his decision intelligently.

The Sabbath will be the great test of loyalty, for it is the point of truth especially controverted. When the final test shall be brought to bear upon men, then the line of distinction will be drawn between those who serve God and those who serve Him not. While the observance of the false sabbath in compliance with the law of the state, contrary to the fourth commandment, will be an avowal of allegiance to a power that is in opposition to God, the keeping of the true Sabbath, in obedience to God's law, is an evidence of loyalty to the Creator. While one class, by accepting the sign of submission to earthly powers, receives the mark of the beast, the other choosing the token of allegiance to divine authority, receive the seal of God.

Heretofore those who presented the truths of the third angel's message have often been regarded as mere alarmists. Their predictions that religious intolerance would gain control in the United States, that church and state would unite to persecute those who keep the commandments of God, have been pronounced groundless and absurd. It has been confidently declared that this land could never become other than what it has been—the defender of religious freedom. But as the question of enforcing Sunday observance is widely agitated, the event so long doubted and disbelieved is seen to be approaching, and the third message will produce an effect which it could not have had before.

In every generation God has sent His servants to rebuke sin, both in the world and in the church. But the people desire smooth things spoken to them, and the pure, unvarnished truth is not acceptable. Many reformers, in entering upon their work, determined to exercise great prudence in attacking the sins of the church and the nation. They hoped, by the example of a pure Christian life, to lead the people back to the doctrines of the Bible. But the Spirit of God came upon them as it came upon Elijah, moving him to rebuke the sins of a wicked king and an apostate people; they could not refrain from preaching the plain utterances of the Bible— doctrines which they had been reluctant to present. They were impelled to zealously declare the truth and the danger which threatened souls. The words which the Lord gave them they uttered, fearless of consequences, and the people were compelled to hear the warning.

Thus the message of the third angel will be proclaimed. As the time comes for it to be given with greatest power, the Lord will work through humble instruments, leading the minds of those who consecrate themselves to His service. The laborers will be qualified rather by the unction of His Spirit than by the training of literary institutions. Men of faith and prayer will be constrained to go forth with holy zeal, declaring the words which God gives them. The sins of Babylon will be laid open. The fearful results of enforcing the observances of the church by civil authority, the inroads of spiritualism, the stealthy but rapid progress of the papal power—all will be unmasked. By these solemn warnings the people will be stirred. Thousands upon thousands will listen who have never heard words like these. In amazement they hear the testimony that Babylon is the church, fallen because of her errors and sins, because of her rejection of the truth sent to her from heaven.

As the people go to their former teachers with the eager inquiry, Are these things so? the ministers present fables, prophesy smooth things, to soothe their fears and quiet the awakened conscience. But since many refuse to be satisfied with the mere authority of men and demand a plain "Thus saith the Lord", the popular ministry, like the Pharisees of old, filled with anger as their authority is questioned, will denounce the message as of Satan and stir up the sin-loving multitudes to revile and persecute those who proclaim it.

As the controversy extends into new fields and the minds of the people are called to God's downtrodden law, Satan is astir. The power attending the message will only madden those who oppose it. The clergy will put forth almost superhuman efforts to shut away the light lest it should shine upon their flocks. By every means at their command they will endeavor to suppress the discussion of these vital questions. The church appeals to the strong arm of civil power, and, in this work, papists and Protestants unite. As the movement for Sunday enforcement becomes more bold and decided, the law will be invoked against commandment keepers. They will be threatened with fines and imprisonment, and some will be offered positions of influence, and other rewards and advantages, as inducements to renounce their faith. But their steadfast answer is: "Show us from the word of God our error"—the same plea that was made by Luther under similar circumstances. Those who are arraigned before the courts make a strong vindication of the truth, and some who hear them are led to take their stand to keep all the commandments of God. Thus light will be brought before thousands who otherwise would know nothing of these truths.

Conscientious obedience to the word of God will be treated as rebellion. Blinded by Satan, the parent will exercise harshness and severity toward the believing child; the master or mistress will oppress the commandment-keeping servant. Affection will be alienated; children will be disinherited and driven from home. The words of Paul will be literally fulfilled: "All that will live godly in Christ Jesus shall suffer persecution." 2 Timothy 3:12. As the defenders of truth refuse to honor the Sunday-sabbath, some of them will be thrust into prison, some will be exiled, some will be treated as slaves. To human wisdom all this now seems impossible; but as the restraining Spirit of God shall be withdrawn from men, and they shall be under the control of Satan, who hates the divine precepts, there will be strange developments. The heart can be very cruel when God's fear and love are removed.

As the storm approaches, a large class who have professed faith in the third angel's message, but have not been sanctified through obedience to the truth, abandon their position and join the ranks of the opposition. By uniting with the world and partaking of its spirit, they have come to view matters in nearly the same light; and when the test is brought, they are prepared to choose the easy, popular side. Men of talent and pleasing address, who once rejoiced in the truth, employ their powers to deceive and mislead souls. They become the most bitter enemies of their former brethren. When Sabbath keepers are brought before the courts to answer for their faith, these apostates are the most efficient agents of Satan to misrepresent and accuse them, and by false reports and insinuations to stir up the rulers against them.

In this time of persecution the faith of the Lord's servants will be tried. They have faithfully given the warning, looking to God and to His word alone. God's Spirit, moving upon their hearts, has constrained them to speak. Stimulated with holy zeal, and with the divine impulse strong upon them, they entered upon the performance of their duties without coldly calculating the consequences of speaking to the people the word which the Lord had given them. They have not consulted their temporal interests, nor sought to preserve their reputation or their lives. Yet when the storm of opposition and reproach bursts upon them, some, overwhelmed with consternation, will be ready to exclaim: "Had we foreseen the consequences of our words, we would have held our peace." They are hedged in with difficulties. Satan assails them with fierce temptations. The work which they have undertaken seems far beyond their ability to accomplish. They are threatened with destruction. The enthusiasm which animated them is gone; yet they cannot turn back. Then, feeling their utter helplessness, they flee to the Mighty One for strength. They remember that the words which they have spoken were not theirs, but His who bade them give the warning. God put the truth into their hearts, and they could not forbear to proclaim it.

The same trials have been experienced by men of God in ages past. Wycliffe, Huss, Luther, Tyndale, Baxter, Wesley, urged that all doctrines be brought to the test of the Bible and declared that they would renounce everything which it condemned. Against these men persecution raged with relentless fury; yet they ceased not to declare the truth. Different periods in the history of the church have each been marked by the development of some special truth, adapted to the necessities of God's people at that time. Every new truth has made its way against hatred and opposition; those who were blessed with its light were tempted and tried. The Lord gives a special truth for the people in an emergency. Who dare refuse to publish it? He commands His servants to present the last invitation of mercy to the world. They cannot remain silent, except at the peril of their souls. Christ's ambassadors have nothing to do with consequences. They must perform their duty and leave results with God.

As the opposition rises to a fiercer height, the servants of God are again perplexed; for it seems to them that they have brought the crisis. But conscience and the word of God assure them that their course is right; and although the trials continue, they are strengthened to bear them. The contest grows closer and sharper, but their faith and courage rise with the emergency. Their testimony is: "We dare not tamper with God's word, dividing His holy law; calling one portion essential and another nonessential, to gain the favor of the world. The Lord whom we serve is able to deliver us. Christ has conquered the powers of earth; and shall we be afraid of a world already conquered?"

Persecution in its varied forms is the development of a principle which will exist as long as Satan exists and Christianity has vital power. No man can serve God without enlisting against himself the opposition of the hosts of darkness. Evil angels will assail him, alarmed that his influence is taking the prey from their hands. Evil men, rebuked by his example, will unite with them in seeking to separate him from God by alluring temptations. When these do not succeed, then a compelling power is employed to force the conscience.

But so long as Jesus remains man's intercessor in the sanctuary above, the restraining influence of the Holy Spirit is felt by rulers and people. It still controls to some extent the laws of the land. Were it not for these laws, the condition of the world would be much worse than it now is. While many of our rulers are active agents of Satan, God also has His agents among the leading men of the nation. The enemy moves upon his servants to propose measures that would greatly impede the work of God; but statesmen who fear the Lord are influenced by holy angels to oppose such propositions with unanswerable arguments. Thus a few men will hold in check a powerful current of evil. The opposition of the enemies of truth will be restrained that the third angel's message may do its work. When the final warning shall be given, it will arrest the attention of these leading men through whom the Lord is now working, and some of them will accept it, and will stand with the people of God through the time of trouble.

The angel who unites in the proclamation of the third angel's message is to lighten the whole earth with his glory. A work of world-wide extent and unwonted power is here foretold. The advent movement of 1840-44 was a glorious manifestation of the power of God; the first angel's message was carried to every missionary station in the world, and in some countries there was the greatest religious interest which has been witnessed in any land since the Reformation of the sixteenth century; but these are to be exceeded by the mighty movement under the last warning of the third angel.

The work will be similar to that of the Day of Pentecost. As the "former rain" was given, in the outpouring of the Holy Spirit at the opening of the gospel, to cause the upspringing of the precious seed, so the "latter rain"will be given at its close for the ripening of the harvest. "Then shall we know, if we follow on to know the Lord: His going forth is prepared as the morning; and He shall come unto us as the rain, as the latter and former rain unto the earth" (Hosea 6:3). "Be glad then, ye children of Zion, and rejoice in the Lord your God: for He hath given you the former rain moderately, and He will cause to come down for you the rain, the former rain, and the latter rain". (Joel 2:23). "In the last days, saith God, I will pour out of My Spirit upon all flesh…And it shall come to pass, that whosoever shall call on the name of the Lord shall be saved" (Acts 2:17, 21).

The great work of the gospel is not to close with less manifestation of the power of God than marked its opening. The prophecies which were fulfilled in the outpouring of the former rain at the opening of the gospel are again to be fulfilled in the latter rain at its close. Here are "the times of refreshing" to which the apostle Peter looked forward when he said: "Repent ye therefore, and be converted, that your sins may be blotted out, when the times of refreshing shall come from the presence of the Lord; and He shall send Jesus" (Acts 3:19, 20).

Servants of God, with their faces lighted up and shining with holy consecration, will hasten from place to place to proclaim the message from heaven. By thousands of voices, all over the earth, the warning will be given. Miracles will be wrought, the sick will be healed, and signs and wonders will follow the believers. Satan also works, with lying wonders, even bringing down fire from heaven in the sight of men (Revelation 13:13). Thus the inhabitants of the earth will be brought to take their stand.

The message will be carried not so much by argument as by the deep conviction of the Spirit of God. The arguments have been presented. The seed has been sown, and now it will spring up and bear fruit. The publications distributed by missionary workers have exerted their influence, yet many whose minds were impressed have been prevented from fully comprehending the truth or from yielding obedience. Now the rays of light penetrate everywhere, the truth is seen in its clearness, and the honest children of God sever the bands which have held them. Family connections, church relations, are powerless to stay them now. Truth is more precious than all besides. Notwithstanding the agencies combined against the truth, a large number take their stand upon the Lord's side.

CHAPTER 12

The Time of Trouble

"At that time shall Michael stand up, the great Prince which standeth for the children of thy people: and there shall be a time of trouble, such as never was since there was a nation even to that same time: and at that time thy people shall be delivered, everyone that shall be found written in the book" (Daniel 12:1).

When the third angel's message closes, mercy no longer pleads for the guilty inhabitants of the earth. The people of God have accomplished their work. They have received "the latter rain", "the refreshing from the presence of the Lord", and they are prepared for the trying hour before them. Angels are hastening to and fro in heaven. An angel returning from the earth announces that his work is done; the final test has been brought upon the world, and all who have proved themselves loyal to the divine precepts have received "the seal of the living God". Then Jesus ceases His intercession in the sanctuary above. He lifts His hands and with a loud voice says, "It is done;" and all the angelic host lay off their crowns as He makes the solemn announcement: "He that is unjust, let him be unjust still: and he which is filthy, let him be filthy still: and he that is righteous, let him be righteous still: and he that is holy, let him be holy still" (Revelation 22:11). Every case has been decided for life or death. Christ has made the atonement for His people and blotted out their sins. The number of His subjects is made up; "the kingdom and dominion, and the greatness of the kingdom under the whole heaven," is about to be given to the heirs of salvation, and Jesus is to reign as King of kings and Lord of lords.

When He leaves the sanctuary, darkness covers the inhabitants of the earth. In that fearful time the righteous must live in the sight of a holy God without an intercessor. The restraint which has been upon the wicked is removed, and Satan has entire control of the finally impenitent. God's long-suffering has ended. The world has rejected His mercy, despised His love, and trampled upon His law. The wicked have passed the boundary of their probation; the Spirit of God, persistently resisted, has been at last withdrawn. Unsheltered by divine grace, they have no protection from the wicked one. Satan will then plunge the inhabitants of the earth into one great, final trouble. As the angels of God cease to hold in check the fierce winds of human passion, all the elements of strife will be let loose. The whole world will be involved in ruin more terrible than that which came upon Jerusalem of old.

A single angel destroyed all the first-born of the Egyptians and filled the land with mourning. When David offended against God by numbering the people, one angel caused that terrible destruction by which his sin was punished. The same destructive power exercised by holy angels when God commands, will be exercised by evil angels when He permits. There are forces now ready, and only waiting the divine permission, to spread desolation everywhere.

Those who honor the law of God have been accused of bringing judgments upon the world, and they will be regarded as the cause of the fearful convulsions of nature and the strife and bloodshed among men that are filling the earth with woe. The power attending the last warning has enraged the wicked; their anger is kindled against all who have received the message, and Satan will excite to still greater intensity the spirit of hatred and persecution.

When God's presence was finally withdrawn from the Jewish nation, priests and people knew it not. Though under the control of Satan, and swayed by the most horrible and malignant passions, they still regarded themselves as the chosen of God. The ministration in the temple continued; sacrifices were offered upon its polluted altars, and daily the divine blessing was invoked upon a people guilty of the blood of God's dear Son and seeking to slay His ministers and apostles. So when the irrevocable decision of the sanctuary has been pronounced and the destiny of the world has been forever fixed, the inhabitants of the earth will know it not. The forms of religion will be continued by a people from whom the Spirit of God has been finally withdrawn; and the satanic zeal with which the prince of evil will inspire them for the accomplishment of his malignant designs, will bear the semblance of zeal for God.

As the Sabbath has become the special point of controversy throughout Christendom, and religious and secular authorities have combined to enforce the observance of the Sunday, the persistent refusal of a small minority to yield to the popular demand will make them objects of universal execration. It will be urged that the few who stand in opposition to an institution of the church and a law of the state ought not to be tolerated; that it is better for them to suffer than for whole nations to be thrown into confusion and lawlessness. The same argument eighteen hundred years ago was brought against Christ by the "rulers of the people". "It is expedient for us", said the wily Caiaphas, "that one man should die for the people, and that the whole nation perish not" (John 11:50). This argument will appear conclusive; and a decree will finally be issued against those who hallow the Sabbath of the fourth commandment, denouncing them as deserving of the severest punishment and giving the people liberty, after a certain time, to put them to death. Romanism in the Old World and apostate Protestantism in the New will pursue a similar course toward those who honor all the divine precepts.

The people of God will then be plunged into those scenes of affliction and distress described by the prophet as the time of Jacob's trouble. "Thus saith the Lord: We have heard a voice of trembling, of fear, and not of peace. . . . All faces are turned into paleness. Alas! for that day is great, so that none is like it: it is even the time of Jacob's trouble; but he shall be saved out of it" (Jeremiah 30:5-7).

Jacob's night of anguish, when he wrestled in prayer for deliverance from the hand of Esau (Genesis 32:24-30), represents the experience of God's people in the time of trouble. Because of the deception practiced to secure his father's blessing, intended for Esau, Jacob had fled for his life, alarmed by his brother's deadly threats. After remaining for many years an exile, he had set out, at God's command, to return with his wives and children, his flocks and herds, to his native country. On reaching the borders of the land, he was filled with terror by the tidings of Esau's approach at the head of a band of warriors, doubtless bent upon revenge. Jacob's company, unarmed and defenseless, seemed about to fall helpless victims of violence and slaughter. And to the burden of anxiety and fear was added the crushing weight of self-reproach, for it was his own sin that had brought this danger. His only hope was in the mercy of God; his only defense must be prayer. Yet he leaves nothing undone on his own part to atone for the wrong to his brother and to avert the threatened danger.

So should the followers of Christ, as they approach the time of trouble, make every exertion to place themselves in a proper light before the people, to disarm prejudice, and to avert the danger which threatens liberty of conscience. Having sent his family away, that they may not witness his distress, Jacob remains alone to intercede with God. He confesses his sin and gratefully acknowledges the mercy of God toward him while with deep humiliation he pleads the covenant made with his fathers and the promises to himself in the night vision at Bethel and in the land of his exile. The crisis in his life has come; everything is at stake. In the darkness and solitude he continues praying and humbling himself before God. Suddenly a hand is laid upon his shoulder. He thinks that an enemy is seeking his life, and with all the energy of despair he wrestles with his assailant.

As the day begins to break, the stranger puts forth his superhuman power; at his touch the strong man seems paralyzed, and he falls, a helpless, weeping suppliant, upon the neck of his mysterious antagonist. Jacob knows now that it is the Angel of the covenant with whom he has been in conflict. Though disabled and suffering the keenest pain, he does not relinquish his purpose. Long has he endured perplexity, remorse, and trouble for his sin; now he must have the assurance that it is pardoned. The divine visitant seems about to depart; but Jacob clings to Him, pleading for a blessing. The Angel urges, "Let Me go, for the day breaketh"; but the patriarch exclaims, "I will not let Thee go, except Thou bless me" (Genesis 32:26). What confidence, what firmness and perseverance, are here displayed! Had this been a boastful, presumptuous claim, Jacob would have been instantly destroyed; but his was the assurance of one who confesses his weakness and unworthiness, yet trusts the mercy of a covenant-keeping God.

"He had power over the Angel, and prevailed" (Hosea 12:4). Through humiliation, repentance, and self-surrender, this sinful, erring mortal prevailed with the Majesty of heaven. He had fastened his trembling grasp upon the promises of God, and the heart of Infinite Love could not turn away the sinner's plea. As an evidence of his triumph and an encouragement to others to imitate his example, his name was changed from one which was a reminder of his sin, to one that commemorated his victory. And the fact that Jacob had prevailed with God was an assurance that he would prevail with men. He no longer feared to encounter his brother's anger, for the Lord was his defense.

Satan had accused Jacob before the angels of God, claiming the right to destroy him because of his sin; he had moved upon Esau to march against him; and during the patriarch's long night of wrestling, Satan endeavored to force upon him a sense of his guilt in order to discourage him and break his hold upon God. Jacob was driven almost to despair; but he knew that without help from heaven he must perish. He had sincerely repented of his great sin, and he appealed to the mercy of God. He would not be turned from his purpose, but held fast the Angel and urged his petition with earnest, agonizing cries until he prevailed.

As Satan influenced Esau to march against Jacob, so he will stir up the wicked to destroy God's people in the time of trouble. And as he accused Jacob, he will urge his accusations against the people of God. He numbers the world as his subjects; but the little company who keep the commandments of God are resisting his supremacy. If he could blot them from the earth, his triumph would be complete. He sees that holy angels are guarding them, and he infers that their sins have been pardoned; but he does not know that their cases have been decided in the sanctuary above. He has an accurate knowledge of the sins which he has tempted them to commit, and he presents these before God in the most exaggerated light, representing this people to be just as deserving as himself of exclusion from the favor of God. He declares that the Lord cannot in justice forgive their sins and yet destroy him and his angels. He claims them as his prey and demands that they be given into his hands to destroy.

As Satan accuses the people of God on account of their sins, the Lord permits him to try them to the uttermost. Their confidence in God, their faith and firmness, will be severely tested. As they review the past, their hopes sink; for in their whole lives they can see little good. They are fully conscious of their weakness and unworthiness. Satan endeavors to terrify them with the thought that their cases are hopeless, that the stain of their defilement will never be washed away. He hopes so to destroy their faith that they will yield to his temptations and turn from their allegiance to God.

Though God's people will be surrounded by enemies who are bent upon their destruction, yet the anguish which they suffer is not a dread of persecution for the truth's sake; they fear that every sin has not been repented of, and that through some fault in themselves they will fail to realize the fulfillment of the Saviour's promise: "I will keep thee from the hour of temptation, which shall come upon all the world" (Revelation 3:10). If they could have the assurance of pardon they would not shrink from torture or death; but should they prove unworthy, and lose their lives because of their own defects of character, then God's holy name would be reproached.

On every hand they hear the plottings of treason and see the active working of rebellion; and there is aroused within them an intense desire, an earnest yearning of soul, that this great apostasy may be terminated and the wickedness of the wicked may come to an end. But while they plead with God to stay the work of rebellion, it is with a keen sense of self-reproach that they themselves have no more power to resist and urge back the mighty tide of evil. They feel that had they always employed all their ability in the service of Christ, going forward from strength to strength, Satan's forces would have less power to prevail against them.

They afflict their souls before God, pointing to their past repentance of their many sins, and pleading the Saviour's promise: "Let him take hold of My strength, that he may make peace with Me; and he shall make peace with Me" (Isaiah 27:5). Their faith does not fail because their prayers are not immediately answered. Though suffering the keenest anxiety, terror, and distress, they do not cease their intercessions. They lay hold of the strength of God as Jacob laid hold of the Angel; and the language of their souls is: "I will not let Thee go, except Thou bless me".

Had not Jacob previously repented of his sin in obtaining the birthright by fraud, God would not have heard his prayer and mercifully preserved his life. So, in the time of trouble, if the people of God had unconfessed sins to appear before them while tortured with fear and anguish, they would be overwhelmed; despair would cut off their faith, and they could not have confidence to plead with God for deliverance. But while they have a deep sense of their unworthiness, they have no concealed wrongs to reveal. Their sins have gone beforehand to judgment and have been blotted out, and they cannot bring them to remembrance.

Satan leads many to believe that God will overlook their unfaithfulness in the minor affairs of life; but the Lord shows in His dealings with Jacob that He will in no wise sanction or tolerate evil. All who endeavor to excuse or conceal their sins, and permit them to remain upon the books of heaven, unconfessed and unforgiven, will be overcome by Satan. The more exalted their profession and the more honorable the position which they hold, the more grievous is their course in the sight of God and the more sure the triumph of their great adversary. Those who delay a preparation for the day of God cannot obtain it in the time of trouble or at any subsequent time. The case of all such is hopeless.

Those professed Christians who come up to that last fearful conflict unprepared will, in their despair, confess their sins in words of burning anguish, while the wicked exult over their distress. These confessions are of the same character as was that of Esau or of Judas. Those who make them, lament the result of transgression, but not its guilt. They feel no true contrition, no abhorrence of evil. They acknowledge their sin, through fear of punishment; but, like Pharaoh of old, they would return to their defiance of Heaven should the judgments be removed.

Jacob's history is also an assurance that God will not cast off those who have been deceived and tempted and betrayed into sin, but who have returned unto Him with true repentance. While Satan seeks to destroy this class, God will send His angels to comfort and protect them in the time of peril. The assaults of Satan are fierce and determined, his delusions are terrible; but the Lord's eye is upon His people, and His ear listens to their cries. Their affliction is great, the flames of the furnace seem about to consume them; but the Refiner will bring them forth as gold tried in the fire. God's love for His children during the period of their severest trial is as strong and tender as in the days of their sunniest prosperity; but it is needful for them to be placed in the furnace of fire; their earthliness must be consumed, that the image of Christ may be perfectly reflected.

The season of distress and anguish before us will require a faith that can endure weariness, delay, and hunger—a faith that will not faint though severely tried. The period of probation is granted to all to prepare for that time. Jacob prevailed because he was persevering and determined. His victory is an evidence of the power of importunate prayer. All who will lay hold of God's promises, as he did, and be as earnest and persevering as he was, will succeed as he succeeded. Those who are unwilling to deny self, to agonize before God, to pray long and earnestly for His blessing, will not obtain it. Wrestling with God—how few know what it is! How few have ever had their souls drawn out after God with intensity of desire until every power is on the stretch. When waves of despair which no language can express sweep over the suppliant, how few cling with unyielding faith to the promises of God.

Those who exercise but little faith now, are in the greatest danger of falling under the power of satanic delusions and the decree to compel the conscience. And even if they endure the test they will be plunged into deeper distress and anguish in the time of trouble, because they have never made it a habit to trust in God. The lessons of faith which they have neglected they will be forced to learn under a terrible pressure of discouragement.

We should now acquaint ourselves with God by proving His promises. Angels record every prayer that is earnest and sincere. We should rather dispense with selfish gratifications than neglect communion with God. The deepest poverty, the greatest self-denial, with His approval, is better than riches, honors, ease, and friendship without it. We must take time to pray. If we allow our minds to be absorbed by worldly interests, the Lord may give us time by removing from us our idols of gold, of houses, or of fertile lands.

The young would not be seduced into sin if they would refuse to enter any path save that upon which they could ask God's blessing. If the messengers who bear the last solemn warning to the world would pray for the blessing of God, not in a cold, listless, lazy manner, but fervently and in faith, as did Jacob, they would find many places where they could say: "I have seen God face to face, and my life is preserved" (Genesis 32:30). They would be accounted of heaven as princes, having power to prevail with God and with men.

The "time of trouble, such as never was" is soon to open upon us; and we shall need an experience which we do not now possess and which many are too indolent to obtain. It is often the case that trouble is greater in anticipation than in reality; but this is not true of the crisis before us. The most vivid presentation cannot reach the magnitude of the ordeal. In that time of trial, every soul must stand for himself before God. "Though Noah, Daniel, and Job were in the land, as I live, saith the Lord God, they shall deliver neither son nor daughter; they shall but deliver their own souls by their righteousness" (Ezekiel 14:20).

Now, while our great High Priest is making the atonement for us, we should seek to become perfect in Christ. Not even by a thought could our Saviour be brought to yield to the power of temptation. Satan finds in human hearts some point where he can gain a foothold; some sinful desire is cherished, by means of which his temptations assert their power. But Christ declared of Himself: "The prince of this world cometh, and hath nothing in Me" (John 14:30. Satan could find nothing in the Son of God that would enable him to gain the victory. He had kept His Father's commandments, and there was no sin in Him that Satan could use to his advantage. This is the condition in which those must be found who shall stand in the time of trouble.

It is in this life that we are to separate sin from us, through faith in the atoning blood of Christ. Our precious Saviour invites us to join ourselves to Him, to unite our weakness to His strength, our ignorance to His wisdom, our unworthiness to His merits. God's providence is the school in which we are to learn the meekness and lowliness of Jesus. The Lord is ever setting before us, not the way we would choose, which seems easier and pleasanter to us, but the true aims of life. It rests with us to co-operate with the agencies which Heaven employs in the work of conforming our characters to the divine model. None can neglect or defer this work but at the most fearful peril to their souls.

The apostle John in vision heard a loud voice in heaven exclaiming: "Woe to the inhabiters of the earth and of the sea! for the devil is come down unto you, having great wrath, because he knoweth that he hath but a short time". (Revelation 12:12). Fearful are the scenes which call forth this exclamation from the heavenly voice. The wrath of Satan increases as his time grows short, and his work of deceit and destruction will reach its culmination in the time of trouble.

Fearful sights of a supernatural character will soon be revealed in the heavens, in token of the power of miracle-working demons. The spirits of devils will go forth to the kings of the earth and to the whole world, to fasten them in deception, and urge them on to unite with Satan in his last struggle against the government of heaven. By these agencies, rulers and subjects will be alike deceived. Persons will arise pretending to be Christ Himself, and claiming the title and worship which belong to the world's Redeemer. They will perform wonderful miracles of healing and will profess to have revelations from heaven contradicting the testimony of the Scriptures.

As the crowning act in the great drama of deception, Satan himself will personate Christ. The church has long professed to look to the Saviour's advent as the consummation of her hopes. Now the great deceiver will make it appear that Christ has come. In different parts of the earth, Satan will manifest himself among men as a majestic being of dazzling brightness, resembling the description of the Son of God given by John in the Revelation (Revelation 1:13-15). The glory that surrounds him is unsurpassed by anything that mortal eyes have yet beheld. The shout of triumph rings out upon the air: "Christ has come! Christ has come!" The people prostrate themselves in adoration before him, while he lifts up his hands and pronounces a blessing upon them, as Christ blessed His disciples when He was upon the earth. His voice is soft and subdued, yet full of melody. In gentle, compassionate tones he presents some of the same gracious, heavenly truths which the Saviour uttered; he heals the diseases of the people, and then, in his assumed character of Christ, he claims to have changed the Sabbath to Sunday, and commands all to hallow the day which he has blessed. He declares that those who persist in keeping holy the seventh day are blaspheming his name by refusing to listen to his angels sent to them with light and truth. This is the strong, almost overmastering delusion. Like the Samaritans who were deceived by Simon Magus, the multitudes, from the least to the greatest, give heed to these sorceries, saying: This is "the great power of God" (Acts 8:10).

But the people of God will not be misled. The teachings of this false christ are not in accordance with the Scriptures. His blessing is pronounced upon the worshipers of the beast and his image, the very class upon whom the Bible declares that God's unmingled wrath shall be poured out. And, furthermore, Satan is not permitted to counterfeit the manner of Christ's advent. The Saviour has warned His people against deception upon this point, and has clearly foretold the manner of His second coming. "There shall arise false christs, and false prophets, and shall show great signs and wonders; insomuch that, if it were possible, they shall deceive the very elect. . . . Wherefore if they shall say unto you, Behold, He is in the desert; go not forth; behold, He is in the secret chambers; believe it not. For as the lightning cometh out of the east, and shineth even unto the west; so shall also the coming of the Son of man be" (Matthew 24:24-27, 31; 25:31; Revelation 1:7; 1 Thessalonians 4:16, 17). This coming there is no possibility of counterfeiting. It will be universally known—witnessed by the whole world.

Only those who have been diligent students of the Scriptures and who have received the love of the truth will be shielded from the powerful delusion that takes the world captive. By the Bible testimony these will detect the deceiver in his disguise. To all the testing time will come. By the sifting of temptation the genuine Christian will be revealed. Are the people of God now so firmly established upon His word that they would not yield to the evidence of their senses? Would they, in such a crisis, cling to the Bible and the Bible only? Satan will, if possible, prevent them from obtaining a preparation to stand in that day. He will so arrange affairs as to hedge up their way, entangle them with earthly treasures, cause them to carry a heavy, wearisome burden that their hearts may be overcharged with the cares of this life and the day of trial may come upon them as a thief.

As the decree issued by the various rulers of Christendom against commandment keepers shall withdraw the protection of government and abandon them to those who desire their destruction, the people of God will flee from the cities and villages and associate together in companies, dwelling in the most desolate and solitary places. Many will find refuge in the strongholds of the mountains. Like the Christians of the Piedmont valleys, they will make the high places of the earth their sanctuaries and will thank God for "the munitions of rocks." Isaiah 33:16. But many of all nations and of all classes, high and low, rich and poor, black and white, will be cast into the most unjust and cruel bondage. The beloved of God pass weary days, bound in chains, shut in by prison bars, sentenced to be slain, some apparently left to die of starvation in dark and loathsome dungeons. No human ear is open to hear their moans; no human hand is ready to lend them help.

Will the Lord forget His people in this trying hour? Did He forget faithful Noah when judgments were visited upon the antediluvian world? Did He forget Lot when the fire came down from heaven to consume the cities of the plain? Did He forget Joseph surrounded by idolaters in Egypt? Did He forget Elijah when the oath of Jezebel threatened him with the fate of the prophets of Baal? Did He forget Jeremiah in the dark and dismal pit of his prison house? Did He forget the three worthies in the fiery furnace? or Daniel in the den of lions?

"Zion said, The Lord hath forsaken me, and my Lord hath forgotten me. Can a woman forget her sucking child, that she should not have compassion on the son of her womb? yea, they may forget, yet will I not forget thee. Behold, I have graven thee upon the palms of My hands" (Isaiah 49:14-16). The Lord of hosts has said: "He that toucheth you toucheth the apple of His eye" (Zechariah 2:8).

Though enemies may thrust them into prison, yet dungeon walls cannot cut off the communication between their souls and Christ. One who sees their every weakness, who is acquainted with every trial, is above all earthly powers; and angels will come to them in lonely cells, bringing light and peace from heaven. The prison will be as a palace; for the rich in faith dwell there, and the gloomy walls will be lighted up with heavenly light as when Paul and Silas prayed and sang praises at midnight in the Philippian dungeon.

God's judgments will be visited upon those who are seeking to oppress and destroy His people. His long forbearance with the wicked emboldens men in transgression, but their punishment is nonetheless certain and terrible because it is long delayed. "The Lord shall rise up as in Mount Perazim, He shall be wroth as in the valley of Gibeon, that He may do His work, His strange work; and bring to pass His act, His strange act" (Isaiah 28:21). To our merciful God the act of punishment is a strange act. "As I live, saith the Lord God, I have no pleasure in the death of the wicked" (Ezekiel 33:11). The Lord is "merciful and gracious, long-suffering, and abundant in goodness and truth, .. forgiving iniquity and transgression and sin…Yet He will "by no means clear the guilty…The Lord is slow to anger, and great in power, and will not at all acquit the wicked" (Exodus 34:6, 7; Nahum 1:3). By terrible things in righteousness He will vindicate the authority of His downtrodden law. The severity of the retribution awaiting the transgressor may be judged by the Lord's reluctance to execute justice. The nation with which He bears long, and which He will not smite until it has filled up the measure of its iniquity in God's account, will finally drink the cup of wrath unmixed with mercy.

When Christ ceases His intercession in the sanctuary, the unmingled wrath threatened against those who worship the beast and his image and receive his mark (Revelation 14:9, 10), will be poured out. The plagues upon Egypt when God was about to deliver

Israel were similar in character to those more terrible and extensive judgments which are to fall upon the world just before the final deliverance of God's people. Says the Revelator, in describing those terrific scourges: "There fell a noisome and grievous sore upon the men which had the mark of the beast and upon them which worshiped his image… The sea "became as the blood of a dead man: and every living soul died in the sea. And the rivers and fountains of waters . . . became blood." Terrible as these inflictions are, God's justice stands fully vindicated. The angel of God declares: "Thou art righteous, O Lord, because Thou hast judged thus. For they have shed the blood of saints and prophets, and Thou hast given them blood to drink; for they are worthy" (Revelation 16:2-6). By condemning the people of God to death, they have as truly incurred the guilt of their blood as if it had been shed by their hands. In like manner Christ declared the Jews of His time guilty of all the blood of holy men which had been shed since the days of Abel; for they possessed the same spirit and were seeking to do the same work with these murderers of the prophets.

In the plague that follows, power is given to the sun "to scorch men with fire. And men scorched with great heat" (Verses 8, 9). The prophets thus describe the condition of the earth at this fearful time: "The land mourneth; . . . because the harvest of the field is perished. . . . All the trees of the field are withered: because joy is withered away from the sons of men..The seed is rotten under their clods, the garners are laid desolate. . . . How do the beasts groan! the herds of cattle are perplexed, because they have no pasture. . . . The rivers of water are dried up, and the fire hath devoured the pastures of the wilderness… The songs of the temple shall be howlings in that day, saith the Lord God: there shall be many dead bodies in every place; they shall cast them forth with silence" (Joel 1:10-12, 17-20; Amos 8:3).

These plagues are not universal, or the inhabitants of the earth would be wholly cut off. Yet they will be the most awful scourges that have ever been known to mortals. All the judgments upon men, prior to the close of probation, have been mingled with mercy. The pleading blood of Christ has shielded the sinner from receiving the full measure of his guilt; but in the final judgment, wrath is poured out unmixed with mercy.

In that day, multitudes will desire the shelter of God's mercy which they have so long despised. "Behold, the days come, saith the

Lord God, that I will send a famine in the land, not a famine of bread, nor a thirst for water, but of hearing the words of the Lord: and they shall wander from sea to sea, and from the north even to the east, they shall run to and fro to seek the word of the Lord, and shall not find it" (Amos 8:11, 12).

The people of God will not be free from suffering; but while persecuted and distressed, while they endure privation and suffer for want of food they will not be left to perish. That God who cared for Elijah will not pass by one of His self-sacrificing children. He who numbers the hairs of their head will care for them, and in time of famine they shall be satisfied. While the wicked are dying from hunger and pestilence, angels will shield the righteous and supply their wants. "To him that walketh righteously" is the promise: "Bread shall be given him; his waters shall be sure...When the poor and needy seek water, and there is none, and their tongue faileth for thirst, I the Lord will hear them, I the God of Israel will not forsake them" (Isaiah 33:15, 16; 41:17).

"Although the fig tree shall not blossom, neither shall fruit be in the vines; the labor of the olive shall fail, and the fields shall yield no meat; the flock shall be cut off from the fold, and there shall be no herd in the stalls; yet shall they that fear Him, rejoice in the Lord, and joy in the God of their salvation". (Habakkuk 3:17, 18). "The Lord is thy keeper: the Lord is thy shade upon thy right hand. The sun shall not smite thee by day, nor the moon by night. The Lord shall preserve thee from all evil: He shall preserve thy soul...He shall deliver thee from the snare of the fowler, and from the noisome pestilence. He shall cover thee with His feathers, and under His wings shalt thou trust: His truth shall be thy shield and buckler. Thou shalt not be afraid for the terror by night; nor for the arrow that flieth by day; nor for the pestilence that walketh in darkness; nor for the destruction that wasteth at noonday. A thousand shall fall at thy side, and ten thousand at thy right hand; but it shall not come nigh thee. Only with thine eyes shalt thou behold and see the reward of the wicked. Because thou hast made the Lord, which is my refuge, even the Most High, thy habitation; there shall no evil befall thee, neither shall any plague come nigh thy dwelling" (Psalms 121:5-7; 91:3-10).

Yet to human sight it will appear that the people of God must soon seal their testimony with their blood as did the martyrs before them. They themselves begin to fear that the Lord has left them to fall by the hand of their enemies. It is a time of fearful agony. Day and night they cry unto God for deliverance. The wicked exult, and the jeering cry is heard: "Where now is your faith? Why does not God deliver you out of our hands if you are indeed His people?" But the waiting ones remember Jesus dying upon Calvary's cross and the chief priests and rulers shouting in mockery: "He saved others; Himself He cannot save. If He be the King of Israel, let Him now come down from the cross, and we will believe Him." Matthew 27:42. Like Jacob, all are wrestling with God. Their countenances express their internal struggle. Paleness sits upon every face. Yet they cease not their earnest intercession.

Could men see with heavenly vision, they would behold companies of angels that excel in strength stationed about those who have kept the word of Christ's patience. With sympathizing tenderness, angels have witnessed their distress and have heard their prayers. They are waiting the word of their Commander to snatch them from their peril. But they must wait yet a little longer. The people of God must drink of the cup and be baptized with the baptism. The very delay, so painful to them, is the best answer to their petitions. As they endeavor to wait trustingly for the Lord to work they are led to exercise faith, hope, and patience, which have been too little exercised during their religious experience. Yet for the elect's sake the time of trouble will be shortened. "Shall not God avenge His own elect, which cry day and night unto Him? . . . I tell you that He will avenge them speedily" (Luke 18:7, 8). The end will come more quickly than men expect. The wheat will be gathered and bound in sheaves for the garner of God; the tares will be bound as fagots for the fires of destruction.

The heavenly sentinels, faithful to their trust, continue their watch. Though a general decree has fixed the time when commandment keepers may be put to death, their enemies will in some cases anticipate the decree, and before the time specified, will endeavor to take their lives. But none can pass the mighty guardians stationed about every faithful soul. Some are assailed in their flight from the cities and villages; but the swords raised against them break and fall powerless as a straw. Others are defended by angels in the form of men of war.

In all ages, God has wrought through holy angels for the succor and deliverance of His people. Celestial beings have taken an active part in the affairs of men. They have appeared clothed in garments that shone as the lightning; they have come as men in the garb of wayfarers. Angels have appeared in human form to men of God. They have rested, as if weary, under the oaks at noon. They have accepted the hospitalities of human homes. They have acted as guides to benighted travelers. They have, with their own hands, kindled the fires at the altar. They have opened prison doors and set free the servants of the Lord. Clothed with the panoply of heaven, they came to roll away the stone from the Saviour's tomb.

In the form of men, angels are often in the assemblies of the righteous; and they visit the assemblies of the wicked, as they went to Sodom, to make a record of their deeds, to determine whether they have passed the boundary of God's forbearance. The Lord delights in mercy; and for the sake of a few who really serve Him, He restrains calamities and prolongs the tranquillity of multitudes. Little do sinners against God realize that they are indebted for their own lives to the faithful few whom they delight to ridicule and oppress.

Though the rulers of this world know it not, yet often in their councils angels have been spokesmen. Human eyes have looked upon them; human ears have listened to their appeals; human lips have opposed their suggestions and ridiculed their counsels; human hands have met them with insult and abuse. In the council hall and the court of justice these heavenly messengers have shown an intimate acquaintance with human history; they have proved themselves better able to plead the cause of the oppressed than were their ablest and most eloquent defenders. They have defeated purposes and arrested evils that would have greatly retarded the work of God and would have caused great suffering to His people. In the hour of peril and distress, "the angel of the Lord encampeth round about them that fear Him, and delivereth them" (Psalm 34:7).

With earnest longing, God's people await the tokens of their coming King. As the watchmen are accosted, "What of the night?". The answer is given unfalteringly, "The morning cometh, and also the night" (Isaiah 21:11, 12). Light is gleaming upon the clouds above the mountaintops. Soon there will be a revealing of His glory. The Sun of Righteousness is about to shine forth. The morning and the night are both at hand—the opening of endless day to the righteous, the settling down of eternal night to the wicked."

As the wrestling ones urge their petitions before God, the veil separating them from the unseen seems almost withdrawn. The heavens glow with the dawning of eternal day, and like the melody of angel songs the words fall upon the ear: "Stand fast to your allegiance. Help is coming." Christ, the almighty Victor, holds out to His weary soldiers a crown of immortal glory; and His voice comes from the gates ajar: "Lo, I am with you. Be not afraid. I am acquainted with all your sorrows; I have borne your griefs. You are not warring against untried enemies. I have fought the battle in your behalf, and in My name you are more than conquerors.

The precious Saviour will send help just when we need it. The way to heaven is consecrated by His footprints. Every thorn that wounds our feet has wounded His. Every cross that we are called to bear He has borne before us. The Lord permits conflicts, to prepare the soul for peace. The time of trouble is a fearful ordeal for God's people; but it is the time for every true believer to look up, and by faith he may see the bow of promise encircling him.

"The redeemed of the Lord shall return, and come with singing unto Zion; and everlasting joy shall be upon their head: they shall obtain gladness and joy; and sorrow and mourning shall flee away. I, even I, am He that comforteth you: who art thou, that thou shouldest be afraid of a man that shall die, and of the son of man which shall be made as grass; and forgettest the Lord thy Maker; . . . and hast feared continually every day because of the fury of the oppressor, as if he were ready to destroy? and where is the fury of the oppressor? The captive exile hasteneth that he may be loosed, and that he should not die in the pit, nor that his bread should fail. But I am the Lord thy God, that divided the sea, whose waves roared: The Lord of hosts is His name. And I have put My words in thy mouth, and I have covered thee in the shadow of Mine hand" (Isaiah 51:11-16). "Therefore hear now this, thou afflicted, and drunken, but not with wine: Thus saith thy Lord the Lord, and thy God that pleadeth the cause of His people, Behold, I have taken out of thine hand the cup of trembling, even the dregs of the cup of My fury; thou shalt no more drink it again: but I will put it into the hand of them that afflict thee; which have said to thy soul, Bow down, that we may go over: and thou hast laid thy body as the ground, and as the street, to them that went over" (Verses 21-23).

The eye of God, looking down the ages, was fixed upon the crisis which His people are to meet, when earthly powers shall be arrayed against them. Like the captive exile, they will be in fear of death by starvation or by violence. But the Holy One who divided the Red Sea before Israel, will manifest His mighty power and turn their captivity. "They shall be Mine, saith the Lord of hosts, in that day when I make up My jewels; and I will spare them, as a man spareth his own son that serveth him" (Malachi 3:17). If the blood of Christ's faithful witnesses were shed at this time, it would not, like the blood of the martyrs, be as seed sown to yield a harvest for God. Their fidelity would not be a testimony to convince others of the truth; for the obdurate heart has beaten back the waves of mercy until they return no more.

If the righteous were now left to fall a prey to their enemies, it would be a triumph for the prince of darkness. Says the psalmist: "In the time of trouble He shall hide me in His pavilion: in the secret of His tabernacle shall He hide me" (Psalm 27:5). Christ has spoken: "Come, My people, enter thou into thy chambers, and shut thy doors about thee: hide thyself as it were for a little moment, until the indignation be overpast. For, behold, the Lord cometh out of His place to punish the inhabitants of the earth for their iniquity". (Isaiah 26:20, 21). Glorious will be the deliverance of those who have patiently waited for His coming and whose names are written in the book of life.

CHAPTER 13

God's People Delivered

When the protection of human laws shall be withdrawn from those who honor the law of God, there will be, in different lands, a simultaneous movement for their destruction. As the time appointed in the decree draws near, the people will conspire to root out the hated sect. It will be determined to strike in one night a decisive blow, which shall utterly silence the voice of dissent and reproof.

The people of God—some in prison cells, some hidden in solitary retreats in the forests and the mountains—still plead for divine protection, while in every quarter companies of armed men, urged on by hosts of evil angels, are preparing for the work of death. It is now, in the hour of utmost extremity that the God of Israel will interpose for the deliverance of His chosen. Saith the Lord; "Ye shall have a song, as in the night when a holy solemnity is kept; and gladness of heart, as when one goeth . . . to come into the mountain of the Lord, to the Mighty One of Israel. And the Lord shall cause His glorious voice to be heard, and shall show the lighting down of His arm, with the indignation of His anger, and with the flame of a devouring fire, with scattering, and tempest, and hailstones" (Isaiah 30:29, 30).

With shouts of triumph, jeering, and imprecation, throngs of evil men are about to rush upon their prey, when, lo, a dense blackness, deeper than the darkness of the night, falls upon the earth. Then a rainbow, shining with the glory from the throne of God, spans the heavens and seems to encircle each praying company. The angry multitudes are suddenly arrested. Their mocking cries die away. The objects of their murderous rage are forgotten. With fearful forebodings they gaze upon the symbol of God's covenant and long to be shielded from its overpowering brightness.

By the people of God a voice, clear and melodious, is heard, saying, "Look up" and, lifting their eyes to the heavens, they behold the bow of promise. The black, angry clouds that covered the firmament are parted, and like Stephen they look up steadfastly into heaven and see the glory of God and the Son of man seated upon His throne. In His divine form they discern the marks of His humiliation; and from His lips they hear the request presented before His Father and the holy angels: "I will that they also, whom Thou hast given Me, be with Me where I am" (John 17:24). Again a voice, musical and triumphant, is heard, saying: (They come! they come! holy, harmless, and undefiled. They have kept the word of My patience; they shall walk among the angels; and the pale, quivering lips of those who have held fast their faith utter a shout of victory.

It is at midnight that God manifests His power for the deliverance of His people. The sun appears, shining in its strength. Signs and wonders follow in quick succession. The wicked look with terror and amazement upon the scene; while the righteous behold with solemn joy the tokens of their deliverance. Everything in nature seems turned out of its course. The streams cease to flow. Dark, heavy clouds come up and clash against each other. In the midst of the angry heavens is one clear space of indescribable glory, whence comes the voice of God like the sound of many waters, saying: "It is done" (Revelation 16:17).

That voice shakes the heavens and the earth. There is a mighty earthquake, "such as was not since men were upon the earth, so mighty an earthquake, and so great" (Rrevelation 16: 17, 18). The firmament appears to open and shut. The glory from the throne of God seems flashing through. The mountains shake like a reed in the wind, and ragged rocks are scattered on every side. There is a roar as of a coming tempest. The sea is lashed into fury. There is heard the shriek of a hurricane like the voice of demons upon a mission of destruction. The whole earth heaves and swells like the waves of the sea. Its surface is breaking up. Its very foundations seem to be giving way. Mountain chains are sinking. Inhabited islands disappear. The seaports that have become like Sodom for wickedness are swallowed up by the angry waters. Babylon the great has come in remembrance before God, "to give unto her the cup of the wine of the fierceness of His wrath. " Great hailstones, every one about the weight of a talent," are doing their work of destruction. (Verses 19, 21). The proudest cities of the earth are laid low. The lordly palaces, upon which the world's great men have lavished their wealth in order to glorify themselves, are crumbling to ruin before their eyes. Prison walls are rent asunder, and God's people, who have been held in bondage for their faith, are set free.

Graves are opened, and "many of them that sleep in the dust of the earth. . . awake, some to everlasting life, and some to shame and everlasting contempt" (Daniel 12:2). All who have died in the faith of the third angel's message come forth from the tomb glorified, to hear God's covenant of peace with those who have kept His law. (They also which pierced Him" (Revelation 1:7), those that mocked and derided Christ's dying agonies, and the most violent opposers of His truth and His people, are raised to behold Him in His glory and to see the honor placed upon the loyal and obedient.

Thick clouds still cover the sky; yet the sun now and then breaks through, appearing like the avenging eye of Jehovah. Fierce lightnings leap from the heavens, enveloping the earth in a sheet of flame. Above the terrific roar of thunder, voices, mysterious and awful, declare the doom of the wicked. The words spoken are not comprehended by all; but they are distinctly understood by the false teachers. Those who a little before were so reckless, so boastful and defiant, so exultant in their cruelty to God's commandment-keeping people, are now overwhelmed with consternation and shuddering in fear. Their wails are heard above the sound of the elements. Demons acknowledge the deity of Christ and tremble before His power, while men are supplicating for mercy and groveling in abject terror.

Said the prophets of old, as they beheld in holy vision the day of God: "Howl ye; for the day of the Lord is at hand; it shall come as a destruction from the Almighty" (Isaiah 13:6). "Enter into the rock, and hide thee in the dust, for fear of the Lord, and for the glory of His majesty. The lofty looks of man shall be humbled, and the haughtiness of men shall be bowed down, and the Lord alone shall be exalted in that day. For the day of the Lord of hosts shall be upon everyone that is proud and lofty, and upon everyone that is lifted up; and he shall be brought low...In that day a man shall cast the idols of his silver, and the idols of his gold, which they made each one for himself to worship, to the moles and to the bats; to go into the clefts of the rocks, and into the tops of the ragged rocks, for fear of the Lord, and for the glory of His majesty, when He ariseth to shake terribly the earth" (Isaiah 2:10-12, 20, 21).

Through a rift in the clouds there beams a star whose brilliancy is increased fourfold in contrast with the darkness. It speaks hope and joy to the faithful, but severity and wrath to the transgressors of God's law. Those who have sacrificed all for Christ are now secure, hidden as in the secret of the Lord's pavilion. They have been tested, and before the world and the despisers of truth they have evinced their fidelity to Him who died for them. A marvelous change has come over those who have held fast their integrity in the very face of death. They have been suddenly delivered from the dark and terrible tyranny of men transformed to demons. Their faces, so lately pale, anxious, and haggard, are now aglow with wonder, faith, and love. Their voices rise in triumphant song: "God is our refuge and strength, a very present help in trouble. Therefore will not we fear, though the earth be removed, and though the mountains be carried into the midst of the sea; though the waters thereof roar and be troubled, though the mountains shake with the swelling thereof" (Psalm 46:1-3).

While these words of holy trust ascend to God, the clouds sweep back, and the starry heavens are seen, unspeakably glorious in contrast with the black and angry firmament on either side. The glory of the celestial city streams from the gates ajar. Then there appears against the sky a hand holding two tables of stone folded together. Says the prophet: "The heavens shall declare His righteousness: for God is judge Himself" (Psalm 50:6). That holy law, God's righteousness, that amid thunder and flame was proclaimed from Sinai as the guide of life, is now revealed to men as the rule of judgment. The hand opens the tables, and there are seen the precepts of the Decalogue, traced as with a pen of fire. The words are so plain that all can read them. Memory is aroused, the darkness of superstition and heresy is swept from every mind, and God's ten words, brief, comprehensive, and authoritative, are presented to the view of all the inhabitants of the earth.

It is impossible to describe the horror and despair of those who have trampled upon God's holy requirements. The Lord gave them His law; they might have compared their characters with it and learned their defects while there was yet opportunity for repentance and reform; but in order to secure the favor of the world, they set aside its precepts and taught others to transgress. They have endeavored to compel God's people to profane His Sabbath. Now they are condemned by that law which they have despised. With awful distinctness they see that they are without excuse. They chose whom they would serve and worship. "Then shall ye return, and discern between the righteous and the wicked, between him that serveth God and him that serveth Him not" (Malachi 3:18).

The enemies of God's law, from the ministers down to the least among them, have a new conception of truth and duty. Too late they see that the Sabbath of the fourth commandment is the seal of the living God. Too late they see the true nature of their spurious sabbath and the sandy foundation upon which they have been building. They find that they have been fighting against God. Religious teachers have led souls to perdition while professing to guide them to the gates of Paradise. Not until the day of final accounts will it be known how great is the responsibility of men in holy office and how terrible are the results of their unfaithfulness. Only in eternity can we rightly estimate the loss of a single soul. Fearful will be the doom of him to whom God shall say: Depart, thou wicked servant.

The voice of God is heard from heaven, declaring the day and hour of Jesus' coming, and delivering the everlasting covenant to His people. Like peals of loudest thunder His words roll through the earth. The Israel of God stand listening, with their eyes fixed upward. Their countenances are lighted up with His glory, and shine as did the face of Moses when he came down from Sinai. The wicked cannot look upon them. And when the blessing is pronounced on those who have honored God by keeping His Sabbath holy, there is a mighty shout of victory.

keeping His Sabbath holy, there is a mighty shout of victory.

Soon there appears in the east a small black cloud, about half the size of a man's hand. It is the cloud which surrounds the Saviour and which seems in the distance to be shrouded in darkness. The people of God know this to be the sign of the Son of man. In solemn silence they gaze upon it as it draws nearer the earth, becoming lighter and more glorious, until it is a great white cloud, its base a glory like consuming fire, and above it the rainbow of the covenant. Jesus rides forth as a mighty conqueror. Not now a "Man of Sorrows", to drink the bitter cup of shame and woe, He comes, victor in heaven and earth, to judge the living and the dead. Faithful and True, in righteousness He doth judge and make war... And the armies which were in heaven follow Him" (Revelation 19:11, 14).

With anthems of celestial melody the holy angels, a vast, unnumbered throng, attend Him on His way. The firmament seems filled with radiant forms—"ten thousand times ten thousand, and thousands of thousands. No human pen can portray the scene; no mortal mind is adequate to conceive its splendor. "His glory covered the heavens, and the earth was full of His praise. And His brightness was as the light" (Habakkuk 3:3,4). As the living cloud comes still nearer, every eye beholds the Prince of life. No crown of thorns now mars that sacred head; but a diadem of glory rests on His holy brow. His countenance outshines the dazzling brightness of the noonday sun. "And He hath on His vesture and on His thigh a name written, King of kings, and Lord of lords" (Revelation 19:16).

Before His presence "all faces are turned into paleness". Upon the rejecters of God's mercy falls the terror of eternal despair. "The heart melteth, and the knees smite together, . . . and the faces of them all gather blackness" (Jeremiah 30:6; Nahum 2:10). The righteous cry with trembling: (Who shall be able to stand?" The angels' song is hushed, and there is a period of awful silence. Then the voice of Jesus is heard, saying: "My grace is sufficient for you.". The faces of the righteous are lighted up, and joy fills every heart. And the angels strike a note higher and sing again as they draw still nearer to the earth. The King of kings descends upon the cloud, wrapped in flaming fire. The heavens are rolled together as a scroll, the earth trembles before Him, and every mountain and island is moved out of its place. "Our God shall come, and shall not keep silence: a fire shall devour before Him, and it shall be very tempestuous round about Him. He shall call to the heavens from above, and to the earth, that He may judge His people" (Psalm 50:3, 4).

"And the kings of the earth, and the great men, and the rich men, and the chief captains, and the mighty men, and every bondman, and every freeman, hid themselves in the dens and in the rocks of the mountains; and said to the mountains and rocks, Fall on us, and hide us from the face of Him that sitteth on the throne, and from the wrath of the Lamb: for the great day of His wrath is come; and who shall be able to stand?" (Revelation 6:15-17).

The derisive jests have ceased. Lying lips are hushed into silence. The clash of arms, the tumult of battle, "with confused noise, and garments rolled in blood" (Isaiah 9:5), is stilled. Nought now is heard but the voice of prayer and the sound of weeping and lamentation.

The cry bursts forth from lips so lately scoffing: "The great day of His wrath is come; and who shall be able to stand?" The wicked pray to be buried beneath the rocks of the mountains rather than meet the face of Him whom they have despised and rejected.

That voice which penetrates the ear of the dead, they know. How often have its plaintive, tender tones called them to repentance. How often has it been heard in the touching entreaties of a friend, a brother, a Redeemer. To the rejecters of His grace no other could be so full of condemnation, so burdened with denunciation, as that voice which has so long pleaded: "Turn ye, turn ye from your evil ways; for why will ye die?" Ezekiel 33:11). Oh, that it were to them the voice of a stranger! Says Jesus: "I have called, and ye refused; I have stretched out My hand, and no man regarded; but ye have set at nought all My counsel, and would none of My reproof" (Proverbs 1:24, 25). That voice awakens memories which they would fain blot out—warnings despised, invitations refused, privileges slighted.

There are those who mocked Christ in His humiliation. With thrilling power come to their minds the Sufferer's words, when, adjured by the high priest, He solemnly declared: "Hereafter shall ye see the Son of man sitting on the right hand of power, and coming in the clouds of heaven" (Matthew 26:64). Now they behold Him in His glory, and they are yet to see Him sitting on the right hand of power.

Those who derided His claim to be the Son of God are speechless now. There is the haughty Herod who jeered at His royal title and bade the mocking soldiers crown Him king. There are the very men who with impious hands placed upon His form the purple robe, upon His sacred brow the thorny crown, and in His unresisting hand the mimic scepter, and bowed before Him in blasphemous mockery. The men who smote and spit upon the Prince of life now turn from His piercing gaze and seek to flee from the overpowering glory of His presence. Those who drove the nails through His hands and feet, the soldier who pierced His side, behold these marks with terror and remorse.

With awful distinctness do priests and rulers recall the events of Calvary. With shuddering horror they remember how, wagging their heads in satanic exultation, they exclaimed: "He saved others; Himself He cannot save. If He be the King of Israel, let Him now come down from the cross, and we will believe Him. He trusted in

God; let Him deliver Him now, if He will have (Matthew 27:42, 43).

Vividly they recall the Saviour's parable of the husbandmen who refused to render to their lord the fruit of the vineyard, who abused his servants and slew his son. They remember, too, the sentence which they themselves pronounced: The lord of the vineyard "will miserably destroy those wicked men." In the sin and punishment of those unfaithful men the priests and elders see their own course and their own just doom. And now there rises a cry of mortal agony. Louder than the shout, "Crucify Him, crucify Him", which rang through the streets of Jerusalem, swells the awful, despairing wail, "He is the Son of God! He is the true Messiah!" They seek to flee from the presence of the King of kings. In the deep caverns of the earth, rent asunder by the warring of the elements, they vainly attempt to hide.

In the lives of all who reject truth there are moments when conscience awakens, when memory presents the torturing recollection of a life of hypocrisy and the soul is harassed with vain regrets. But what are these compared with the remorse of that day when "fear cometh as desolation, "when "destruction cometh as a whirlwind!" (Proverbs 1:27). Those who would have destroyed Christ and His faithful people now witness the glory which rests upon them. In the midst of their terror they hear the voices of the saints in joyful strains exclaiming: "Lo, this is our God; we have waited for Him, and He will save us" (Isaiah 25:9).

Amid the reeling of the earth, the flash of lightning, and the roar of thunder, the voice of the Son of God calls forth the sleeping saints. He looks upon the graves of the righteous, then, raising His hands to heaven, He cries: "Awake, awake, awake, ye that sleep in the dust, and arise!" Throughout the length and breadth of the earth the dead shall hear that voice, and they that hear shall live. And the whole earth shall ring with the tread of the exceeding great army of every nation, kindred, tongue, and people. From the prison house of death they come, clothed with immortal glory, crying: "O death, where is thy sting? O grave, where is thy victory?" (1 Corinthians 15:55). And the living righteous and the risen saints unite their voices in a long, glad shout of victory.

All come forth from their graves the same in stature as when they entered the tomb. Adam, who stands among the risen throng, is of lofty height and majestic form, in stature but little below the

Son of God. He presents a marked contrast to the people of later generations; in this one respect is shown the great degeneracy of the race. But all arise with the freshness and vigor of eternal youth. In the beginning, man was created in the likeness of God, not only in character, but in form and feature. Sin defaced and almost obliterated the divine image; but Christ came to restore that which had been lost. He will change our vile bodies and fashion them like unto His glorious body. The mortal, corruptible form, devoid of comeliness, once polluted with sin, becomes perfect, beautiful, and immortal. All blemishes and deformities are left in the grave. Restored to the tree of life in the long-lost Eden, the redeemed will "grow up" (Malachi 4:2) to the full stature of the race in its primeval glory. The last lingering traces of the curse of sin will be removed, and Christ's faithful ones will appear in "the beauty of the Lord our God," in mind and soul and body reflecting the perfect image of their Lord. Oh, wonderful redemption! long talked of, long hoped for, contemplated with eager anticipation, but never fully understood.

The living righteous are changed "in a moment, in the twinkling of an eye" At the voice of God they were glorified; now they are made immortal and with the risen saints are caught up to meet their Lord in the air. Angels "gather together His elect from the four winds, from one end of heaven to the other." Little children are borne by holy angels to their mothers' arms. Friends long separated by death are united, nevermore to part, and with songs of gladness ascend together to the City of God.

On each side of the cloudy chariot are wings, and beneath it are living wheels; and as the chariot rolls upward, the wheels cry, "Holy," and the wings, as they move, cry, "Holy," and the retinue of angels cry, "Holy, holy, holy, Lord God Almighty." And the redeemed shout, "Alleluia!" as the chariot moves onward toward the New Jerusalem.

Before entering the City of God, the Saviour bestows upon His followers the emblems of victory and invests them with the insignia of their royal state. The glittering ranks are drawn up in the form of a hollow square about their King, whose form rises in majesty high above saint and angel, whose countenance beams upon them full of benignant love. Throughout the unnumbered host of the redeemed every glance is fixed upon Him, every eye beholds His glory whose "visage was so marred more than any man, and His form more than the sons of men". Upon the heads of the overcomers, Jesus with His own right hand places the crown of glory. For each there is a crown, bearing his own "new name"(Revelation 2:17), and the inscription, "Holiness to the Lord." In every hand are placed the victor's palm and the shining harp. Then, as the commanding angels strike the note, every hand sweeps the harp strings with skillful touch, awaking sweet music in rich, melodious strains. Rapture unutterable thrills every heart, and each voice is raised in grateful praise: "Unto Him that loved us, and washed us from our sins in His own blood, and hath made us kings and priests unto God and His Father; to Him be glory and dominion forever and ever" (Revelation 1:5, 6).

Before the ransomed throng is the Holy City. Jesus opens wide the pearly gates, and the nations that have kept the truth enter in. There they behold the Paradise of God, the home of Adam in his innocency. Then that voice, richer than any music that ever fell on mortal ear, is heard, saying: "Your conflict is ended" "Come, ye blessed of My Father, inherit the kingdom prepared for you from the foundation of the world".

Now is fulfilled the Saviour's prayer for His disciples: "I will that they also, whom Thou hast given Me, be with Me where I am." "Faultless before the presence of His glory with exceeding joy" (Jude 24), Christ presents to the Father the purchase of His blood, declaring: "Here am I, and the children whom Thou hast given Me" "Those that Thou gavest Me I have kept" (John 17;16). Oh, the wonders of redeeming love! the rapture of that hour when the infinite Father, looking upon the ransomed, shall behold His image, sin's discord banished, its blight removed, and the human once more in harmony with the divine!

With unutterable love, Jesus welcomes His faithful ones to the joy of their Lord. The Saviour's joy is in seeing, in the kingdom of glory, the souls that have been saved by His agony and humiliation. And the redeemed will be sharers in His joy, as they behold, among the blessed, those who have been won to Christ through their prayers, their labors, and their loving sacrifice. As they gather about the great white throne, gladness unspeakable will fill their hearts, when they behold those whom they have won for Christ, and see that one has gained others, and these still others, all brought into the haven of rest, there to lay their crowns at Jesus' feet and praise Him through the endless cycles of eternity.

As the ransomed ones are welcomed to the City of God, there rings out upon the air an exultant cry of adoration. The two Adams are about to meet. The Son of God is standing with outstretched arms to receive the father of our race—the being whom He created, who sinned against his Maker, and for whose sin the marks of the crucifixion are borne upon the Saviour's form. As Adam discerns the prints of the cruel nails, he does not fall upon the bosom of his Lord, but in humiliation casts himself at His feet, crying: "Worthy, worthy is the Lamb that was slain!". Tenderly the Saviour lifts him up and bids him look once more upon the Eden home from which he has so long been exiled.

After his expulsion from Eden, Adam's life on earth was filled with sorrow. Every dying leaf, every victim of sacrifice, every blight upon the fair face of nature, every stain upon man's purity, was a fresh reminder of his sin. Terrible was the agony of remorse as he beheld iniquity abounding, and, in answer to his warnings, met the reproaches cast upon himself as the cause of sin. With patient humility he bore, for nearly a thousand years, the penalty of transgression. Faithfully did he repent of his sin and trust in the merits of the promised Saviour, and he died in the hope of a resurrection. The Son of God redeemed man's failure and fall; and now, through the work of the atonement, Adam is reinstated in his first dominion.

Transported with joy, he beholds the trees that were once his delight—the very trees whose fruit he himself had gathered in the days of his innocence and joy. He sees the vines that his own hands have trained, the very flowers that he once loved to care for. His mind grasps the reality of the scene; he comprehends that this is indeed Eden restored, more lovely now than when he was banished from it. The Saviour leads him to the tree of life and plucks the glorious fruit and bids him eat. He looks about him and beholds a multitude of his family redeemed, standing in the Paradise of God. Then he casts his glittering crown at the feet of Jesus and, falling upon His breast, embraces the Redeemer. He touches the golden harp, and the vaults of heaven echo the triumphant song: "Worthy, worthy, worthy is the Lamb that was slain, and lives again!" The family of Adam takes up the strain and casts their crowns at the Saviour's feet as they bow before Him in adoration.

This reunion is witnessed by the angels who wept at the fall of Adam and rejoiced when Jesus, after His resurrection, ascended to heaven, having opened the grave for all who should believe on His name. Now they behold the work of redemption accomplished, and they unite their voices in the song of praise.

Upon the crystal sea before the throne, that sea of glass as it were mingled with fire,—so resplendent is it with the glory of God,—are gathered the company that have "gotten the victory over the beast, and over his image, and over his mark, and over the number of his name." With the Lamb upon Mount Zion, "having the harps of God," they stand, the hundred and forty and four thousand that were redeemed from among men; and there is heard, as the sound of many waters, and as the sound of a great thunder, "the voice of harpers harping with their harps". And they sing "a new song" before the throne, a song which no man can learn save the hundred and forty and four thousand. It is the song of Moses and the Lamb—a song of deliverance. None but the hundred and forty-four thousand can learn that song; for it is the song of their experience—an experience such as no other company have ever had. "These are they which follow the Lamb whithersoever He goeth" (Revelation 14:4).

These, having been translated from the earth, from among the living, are counted as "the first fruits unto God and to the Lamb". (Revelation 15:2, 3; 14:1-5). "These are they which came out of great tribulation"; they have passed through the time of trouble such as never was since there was a nation; they have endured the anguish of the time of Jacob's trouble; they have stood without an intercessor through the final outpouring of God's judgments. But they have been delivered, for they have "washed their robes, and made them white in the blood of the Lamb…In their mouth was found no guile: for they are without fault before God…Therefore are they before the throne of God, and serve Him day and night in His temple: and He that sitteth on the throne shall dwell among them… They have seen the earth wasted with famine and pestilence, the sun having power to scorch men with great heat, and they themselves have endured suffering, hunger, and thirst. But "they shall hunger no more, neither thirst any more; neither shall the sun light on them, nor any heat. For the Lamb which is in the midst of the throne shall feed them, and shall lead them unto living fountains of waters: and God shall wipe away all tears from their eyes" (Revelation 7:14-17).

In all ages the Saviour's chosen have been educated and disciplined in the school of trial. They walked in narrow paths on earth; they were purified in the furnace of affliction. For Jesus' sake they endured opposition, hatred, calumny. They followed Him through conflicts sore; they endured self-denial and experienced bitter disappointments. By their own painful experience they learned the evil of sin, its power, its guilt, its woe; and they look upon it with abhorrence. A sense of the infinite sacrifice made for its cure humbles them in their own sight and fills their hearts with gratitude and praise which those who have never fallen cannot appreciate. They love much because they have been forgiven much. Having been partakers of Christ's sufferings, they are fitted to be partakers with Him of His glory.

The heirs of God have come from garrets, from hovels, from dungeons, from scaffolds, from mountains, from deserts, from the caves of the earth, from the caverns of the sea. On earth they were "destitute, afflicted, tormented. Millions went down to the grave loaded with infamy because they steadfastly refused to yield to the deceptive claims of Satan. By human tribunals they were adjudged the vilest of criminals. But now, "God is judge Himself"(Psalm 50:6). Now the decisions of earth are reversed. "The rebuke of His people shall He take away" (Isaiah 25:8). "They shall call them, The holy people, The redeemed of the Lord... He hath appointed to give unto them beauty for ashes, the oil of joy for mourning, the garment of praise for the spirit of heaviness" (Isaiah 62:12; 61:3). They are no longer feeble, afflicted, scattered, and oppressed. Henceforth they are to be ever with the Lord. They stand before the throne clad in richer robes than the most honored of the earth have ever worn. They are crowned with diadems more glorious than were ever placed upon the brow of earthly monarchs. The days of pain and weeping are forever ended. The King of glory has wiped the tears from all faces; every cause of grief has been removed. Amid the waving of palm branches they pour forth a song of praise, clear, sweet, and harmonious; every voice takes up the strain, until the anthem swells through the vaults of heaven: "Salvation to our God which sitteth upon the throne, and unto the Lamb." And all the inhabitants of heaven respond in the ascription: "Amen: Blessing, and glory, and wisdom, and thanksgiving, and honor, and power, and might, be unto our God forever and ever" (Revelation 7:10, 12).

In this life we can only begin to understand the wonderful theme of redemption. With our finite comprehension we may consider most earnestly the shame and the glory, the life and the death, the justice and the mercy, that meet in the cross; yet with the utmost stretch of our mental powers we fail to grasp its full significance. The length and the breadth, the depth and the height, of redeeming love are but dimly comprehended. The plan of redemption will not be fully understood, even when the ransomed see as they are seen and know as they are known; but through the eternal ages new truth will continually unfold to the wondering and delighted mind. Though the griefs and pains and temptations of earth are ended and the cause removed, the people of God will ever have a distinct, intelligent knowledge of what their salvation has cost.

The cross of Christ will be the science and the song of the redeemed through all eternity. In Christ glorified they will behold Christ crucified. Never will it be forgotten that He whose power created and upheld the unnumbered worlds through the vast realms of space, the Beloved of God, the Majesty of heaven, He whom cherub and shining seraph delighted to adore—humbled Himself to uplift fallen man; that He bore the guilt and shame of sin, and the hiding of His Father's face, till the woes of a lost world broke His heart and crushed out His life on Calvary's cross. That the Maker of all worlds, the Arbiter of all destinies, should lay aside His glory and humiliate Himself from love to man will ever excite the wonder and adoration of the universe. As the nations of the saved look upon their Redeemer and behold the eternal glory of the Father shining in His countenance; as they behold His throne, which is from everlasting to everlasting, and know that His kingdom is to have no end, they break forth in rapturous song: "Worthy, worthy is the Lamb that was slain, and hath redeemed us to God by His own most precious blood!"

The mystery of the cross explains all other mysteries. In the light that streams from Calvary the attributes of God which had filled us with fear and awe appear beautiful and attractive. Mercy, tenderness, and parental love are seen to blend with holiness, justice, and power. While we behold the majesty of His throne, high and lifted up, we see His character in its gracious manifestations, and comprehend, as never before, the significance of that endearing title, "Our Father."

It will be seen that He who is infinite in wisdom could devise no plan for our salvation except the sacrifice of His Son. The compensation for this sacrifice is the joy of peopling the earth with ransomed beings, holy, happy, and immortal. The result of the Saviour's conflict with the powers of darkness is joy to the redeemed, redounding to the glory of God throughout eternity. And such is the value of the soul that the Father is satisfied with the price paid; and Christ Himself, beholding the fruits of His great sacrifice, is satisfied.

CHAPTER 14

Desolation of the Earth

"Her sins have reached unto heaven, and God hath remembered her iniquities. . . . In the cup which she hath filled fill to her double. How much she hath glorified herself, and lived deliciously, so much torment and sorrow give her: for she saith in her heart, I sit a queen, and am no widow, and shall see no sorrow. Therefore shall her plagues come in one day, death, and mourning, and famine; and she shall be utterly burned with fire: for strong is the Lord God who judgeth her. And the kings of the earth, who have committed fornication and lived deliciously with her, shall bewail her, and lament for her, . . . saying, Alas, alas that great city Babylon, that mighty city! for in one hour is thy judgment come" (Revelation 18:5-10).

"The merchants of the earth, "that have "waxed rich through the abundance of her delicacies shall stand afar off for the fear of her torment, weeping and wailing, and saying, Alas, alas that great city, that was clothed in fine linen, and purple, and scarlet, and decked with gold, and precious stones, and pearls! For in one hour so great riches is come to nought" (Revelation 18:11, 3, 15-17).

Such are the judgments that fall upon Babylon in the day of the visitation of God's wrath. She has filled up the measure of her iniquity; her time has come; she is ripe for destruction. When the voice of God turns the captivity of His people, there is a terrible awakening of those who have lost all in the great conflict of life. While probation continued they were blinded by Satan's deceptions, and they justified their course of sin. The rich prided themselves upon their superiority to those who were less favored; but they had obtained their riches by violation of the law of God. They had neglected to feed the hungry, to clothe the naked, to deal justly, and to love mercy. They had sought to exalt themselves and to obtain the homage of their fellow creatures. Now they are stripped of all that made them great and are left destitute and defenseless. They look with terror upon the destruction of the idols which they preferred before their Maker. They have sold their souls for earthly riches and enjoyments, and have not sought to become rich toward God. The result is, their lives are a failure; their pleasures are now turned to gall, their treasures to corruption. The gain of a lifetime is swept away in a moment. The rich bemoan the destruction of their grand houses, the scattering of their gold and silver. But their lamentations are silenced by the fear that they themselves are to perish with their idols.

The wicked are filled with regret, not because of their sinful neglect of God and their fellow men, but because God has conquered. They lament that the result is what it is; but they do not repent of their wickedness. They would leave no means untried to conquer if they could.

The world sees the very class whom they have mocked and derided, and desired to exterminate, pass unharmed through pestilence, tempest, and earthquake. He who is to the transgressors of His law a devouring fire, is to His people a safe pavilion.

The minister who has sacrificed truth to gain the favor of men now discerns the character and influence of his teachings. It is apparent that the omniscient eye was following him as he stood in the desk, as he walked the streets, as he mingled with men in the various scenes of life. Every emotion of the soul, every line written, every word uttered, every act that led men to rest in a refuge of falsehood, has been scattering seed; and now, in the wretched, lost souls around him, he beholds the harvest.

Saith the Lord: "They have healed the hurt of the daughter of My people slightly, saying, Peace, peace; when there is no peace…With lies ye have made the heart of the righteous sad, whom I have not made sad; and strengthened the hands of the wicked, that he should not return from his wicked way, by promising him life" (Jeremiah 8:11; Ezekiel 13:22).

"Woe be unto the pastors that destroy and scatter the sheep of My pasture! . . . Behold, I will visit upon you the evil of your doings… Howl, ye shepherds, and cry; and wallow yourselves in the ashes, ye principal of the flock: for your days for slaughter and of your dispersions are accomplished; . . . and the shepherds shall have no way to flee, nor the principal of the flock to escape" (Jeremiah 23:1, 2; 25:34, 35).

Ministers and people see that they have not sustained the right relation to God. They see that they have rebelled against the Author of all just and righteous law. The setting aside of the divine precepts gave rise to thousands of springs of evil, discord, hatred, iniquity, until the earth became one vast field of strife, one sink of corruption. This is the view that now appears to those who rejected truth and chose to cherish error. No language can express the longing which the disobedient and disloyal feel for that which they have lost forever—eternal life. Men whom the world has worshiped for their talents and eloquence now see these things in their true light. They realize what they have forfeited by transgression, and they fall at the feet of those whose fidelity they have despised and derided, and confess that God has loved them.

The people see that they have been deluded. They accuse one another of having led them to destruction; but all unite in heaping their bitterest condemnation upon the ministers. Unfaithful pastors have prophesied smooth things; they have led their hearers to make void the law of God and to persecute those who would keep it holy. Now, in their despair, these teachers confess before the world their work of deception. The multitudes are filled with fury. "We are lost!" they cry, "and you are the cause of our ruin;" and they turn upon the false shepherds. The very ones that once admired them most will pronounce the most dreadful curses upon them. The very hands that once crowned them with laurels will be raised for their destruction. The swords which were to slay God's people are now employed to destroy their enemies. Everywhere there is strife and bloodshed.

"A noise shall come even to the ends of the earth; for the Lord hath a controversy with the nations, He will plead with all flesh; He will give them that are wicked to the sword" (Jeremiah 25:31). For six thousand years the great controversy has been in progress; the Son of God and His heavenly messengers have been in conflict with the power of the evil one, to warn, enlighten, and save the children of men. Now all have made their decisions; the wicked have fully united with Satan in his warfare against God. The time has come for God to vindicate the authority of His downtrodden law. Now the controversy is not alone with Satan, but with men. "The Lord hath a controversy with the nations…He will give them that are wicked to the sword."

The mark of deliverance has been set upon those "that sigh and that cry for all the abominations that be done. "Now the angel of death goes forth, represented in Ezekiel's vision by the men with the slaughtering weapons, to whom the command is given: Slay utterly old and young, both maids, and little children, and women: but come not near any man upon whom is the mark; and begin at My sanctuary. Says the prophet: They began at the ancient men which were before the house." (Ezekiel 9:1-6). The work of destruction begins among those who have professed to be the spiritual guardians of the people. The false watchmen are the first to fall. There are none to pity or to spare. Men, women, maidens, and little children perish together.

"The Lord cometh out of His place to punish the inhabitants of the earth for their iniquity: the earth also shall disclose her blood, and shall no more cover her slain" (Isaiah 26:21). "And this shall be the plague wherewith the Lord will smite all the people that have fought against Jerusalem; Their flesh shall consume away while they stand upon their feet, and their eyes shall consume away in their holes, and their tongue shall consume away in their mouth. And it shall come to pass in that day, that a great tumult from the Lord shall be among them; and they shall lay hold everyone on the hand of his neighbor, and his hand shall rise up against the hand of his neighbor" (Zechariah 14:12, 13). In the mad strife of their own fierce passions, and by the awful outpouring of God's unmingled wrath, fall the wicked inhabitants of the earth—priests, rulers, and people, rich and poor, high and low. "And the slain of the Lord shall be at that day from one end of the earth even unto the other end of the earth: they shall not be lamented, neither gathered, nor buried" (Jeremiah 25:33).

At the coming of Christ the wicked are blotted from the face of the whole earth—consumed with the spirit of His mouth and destroyed by the brightness of His glory. Christ takes His people to the City of God, and the earth is emptied of its inhabitants. "Behold, the Lord maketh the earth empty, and maketh it waste, and turneth it upside down, and scattereth abroad the inhabitants thereof…The land shall be utterly emptied, and utterly spoiled: for the Lord hath spoken this word…Because they have transgressed the laws, changed the ordinance, broken the everlasting covenant. Therefore hath the curse devoured the earth, and they that dwell therein are desolate: therefore the inhabitants of the earth are burned" (Isaiah 24:1, 3, 5, 6).

The whole earth appears like a desolate wilderness. The ruins of cities and villages destroyed by the earthquake, uprooted trees, ragged rocks thrown out by the sea or torn out of the earth itself, are scattered over its surface, while vast caverns mark the spot where the mountains have been rent from their foundations.

Now the event takes place foreshadowed in the last solemn service of the Day of Atonement. When the ministration in the holy of holies had been completed, and the sins of Israel had been removed from the sanctuary by virtue of the blood of the sin offering, then the scapegoat was presented alive before the Lord; and in the presence of the congregation the high priest confessed over him "all the iniquities of the children of Israel, and all their transgressions in all their sins, putting them upon the head of the goat." Leviticus 16:21. In like manner, when the work of atonement in the heavenly sanctuary has been completed, then in the presence of God and heavenly angels and the hosts of the redeemed the sins of God's people will be placed upon Satan; he will be declared guilty of all the evil which he has caused them to commit. And as the scapegoat was sent away into a land not inhabited, so Satan will be banished to the desolate earth, an uninhabited and dreary wilderness.

The Revelator foretells the banishment of Satan and the condition of chaos and desolation to which the earth is to be reduced, and he declares that this condition will exist for a thousand years. After presenting the scenes of the Lord's second coming and the destruction of the wicked, the prophecy continues: "I saw an angel come down from heaven, having the key of the bottomless pit and a great chain in his hand. And he laid hold on the dragon, that old serpent, which is the devil, and Satan, and bound him a thousand years, and cast him into the bottomless pit, and shut him up, and set a seal upon him, that he should deceive the nations no more, till the thousand years should be fulfilled: and after that he must be loosed a little season" (Revelation 20:1-3).

That the expression "bottomless pit" represents the earth in a state of confusion and darkness is evident from other scriptures. Concerning the condition of the earth "in the beginning," the Bible record says that it "was without form, and void; and darkness was upon the face of the deep." [THE HEBREW WORD HERE TRANSLATED

"DEEP" IS RENDERED IN THE SEPTUAGINT (GREEK) TRANSLATION OF THE HEBREW OLD TESTAMENT BY THE SAME WORD RENDERED "BOTTOMLESS PIT" IN REVELATION 20:1-3.]

Genesis 1:2. Prophecy teaches that it will be brought back, partially at least, to this condition. Looking forward to the great day of God, the prophet Jeremiah declares: "I beheld the earth, and, lo, it was without form, and void; and the heavens, and they had no light. I beheld the mountains, and, lo, they trembled, and all the hills moved lightly. I beheld, and, lo, there was no man, and all the birds of the heavens were fled. I beheld, and, lo, the fruitful place was a wilderness, and all the cities thereof were broken down" (Jeremiah 4:23-26).

Here is to be the home of Satan with his evil angels for a thousand years. Limited to the earth, he will not have access to other worlds to tempt and annoy those who have never fallen. It is in this sense that he is bound: there are none remaining, upon whom he can exercise his power. He is wholly cut off from the work of deception and ruin which for so many centuries has been his sole delight.

The prophet Isaiah, looking forward to the time of Satan's overthrow, exclaims: "How art thou fallen from heaven, O Lucifer, son of the morning! how art thou cut down to the ground, which didst weaken the nations! . . . Thou hast said in thine heart, I will ascend into heaven, I will exalt my throne above the stars of God: . . . I will be like the Most High. Yet thou shalt be brought down to hell, to the sides of the pit. They that see thee shall narrowly look upon thee, and consider thee, saying, Is this the man that made the earth to tremble, that did shake kingdoms; that made the world as a wilderness, and destroyed the cities thereof; that opened not the house of his prisoners?" (Isaiah 14:12-17).

For six thousand years, Satan's work of rebellion has "made the earth to tremble." He had "made the world as a wilderness, and destroyed the cities thereof." And he "opened not the house of his prisoners." For six thousand years his prison house has received God's people, and he would have held them captive forever; but Christ had broken his bonds and set the prisoners free.

Even the wicked are now placed beyond the power of Satan, and alone with his evil angels he remains to realize the effect of the curse which sin has brought. "The kings of the nations, even all of them, lie in glory, everyone in his own house [the grave]. But thou art cast out of thy grave like an abominable branch. . . . Thou shalt not be joined with them in burial, because thou hast destroyed thy land, and slain thy people" (Isaiah 14:18-20).

For a thousand years, Satan will wander to and fro in the desolate earth to behold the results of his rebellion against the law of God. During this time his sufferings are intense. Since his fall his life of unceasing activity has banished reflection; but he is now deprived of his power and left to contemplate the part which he has acted since first he rebelled against the government of heaven, and to look forward with trembling and terror to the dreadful future when he must suffer for all the evil that he has done and be punished for the sins that he has caused to be committed.

To God's people the captivity of Satan will bring gladness and rejoicing. Says the prophet: "It shall come to pass in the day that Jehovah shall give thee rest from thy sorrow, and from thy trouble, and from the hard service wherein thou wast made to serve, that thou shalt take up this parable against the king of Babylon [here representing Satan], and say, How hath the oppressor ceased! . . . Jehovah hath broken the staff of the wicked, the scepter of the rulers; that smote the peoples in wrath with a continual stroke, that ruled the nations in anger, with a persecution that none restrained" (Isaiah 3-6).

During the thousand years between the first and the second resurrection the judgment of the wicked takes place. The apostle Paul points to this judgment as an event that follows the second advent. "Judge nothing before the time, until the Lord come, who both will bring to light the hidden things of darkness, and will make manifest the counsels of the hearts" (1 Corinthians 4:5). Daniel declares that when the Ancient of Days came, "judgment was given to the saints of the Most High" (Daniel 7:22). At this time the righteous reign as kings and priests unto God. John in the Revelation says: "I saw thrones, and they sat upon them, and judgment was given unto them...They shall be priests of God and of Christ, and shall reign with Him a thousand years" (Revelation 20:4, 6). It is at this time that, as foretold by Paul, "the saints shall judge the world" (1 Corinthians 6:2). In union with Christ they judge the wicked, comparing their acts with the statute book, the Bible, and deciding every case according to the deeds done in the body. Then the portion which the wicked must suffer is meted out, according to their works; and it is recorded against their names in the book of death.

DESOLATION OF THE EARTH

Satan also and evil angels are judged by Christ and His people. Says Paul: "Know ye not that we shall judge angels?" (1Corinthians 6:3). And Jude declares that "the angels which kept not their first estate, but left their own habitation, He hath reserved in everlasting chains under darkness unto the judgment of the great day" (Jude 6).

At the close of the thousand years the second resurrection will take place. Then the wicked will be raised from the dead and appear before God for the execution of "the judgment written" Thus the revelator, after describing the resurrection of the righteous, says: "The rest of the dead lived not again until the thousand years were finished." Revelation 20:5. And Isaiah declares, concerning the wicked: "They shall be gathered together, as prisoners are gathered in the pit, and shall be shut up in the prison, and after many days shall they be visited" (Isaiah 24:22).

CHAPTER 15

The Controversy Ended

At the close of the thousand years, Christ again returns to the earth. He is accompanied by the host of the redeemed and attended by a retinue of angels. As He descends in terrific majesty He bids the wicked dead arise to receive their doom. They come forth, a mighty host, numberless as the sands of the sea. What a contrast to those who were raised at the first resurrection! The righteous were clothed with immortal youth and beauty. The wicked bear the traces of disease and death.

Every eye in that vast multitude is turned to behold the glory of the Son of God. With one voice the wicked hosts exclaim: "Blessed is He that cometh in the name of the Lord!" It is not love to Jesus that inspires this utterance. The force of truth urges the words from unwilling lips. As the wicked went into their graves, so they come forth with the same enmity to Christ and the same spirit of rebellion. They are to have no new probation in which to remedy the defects of their past lives. Nothing would be gained by this. A lifetime of transgression has not softened their hearts. A second probation, were it given them, would be occupied as was the first in evading the requirements of God and exciting rebellion against Him.

Christ descends upon the Mount of Olives, whence, after His resurrection, He ascended, and where angels repeated the promise of His return. Says the prophet: "The Lord my God shall come, and all the saints with Thee." "And His feet shall stand in that day upon the Mount of Olives, which is before Jerusalem on the east, and the Mount of Olives shall cleave in the midst thereof, . . . and there shall be a very great valley...And the Lord shall be king over all the earth: in that day shall there be one Lord, and His name one" (Zechariah

14:5, 4, 9). As the New Jerusalem, in its dazzling splendor, comes down out of heaven, it rests upon the place purified and made ready to receive it, and Christ, with His people and the angels, enters the Holy City.

Now Satan prepares for a last mighty struggle for the supremacy. While deprived of his power and cut off from his work of deception, the prince of evil was miserable and dejected; but as the wicked dead are raised and he sees the vast multitudes upon his side, his hopes revive, and he determines not to yield the great controversy. He will marshal all the armies of the lost under his banner and through them endeavor to execute his plans. The wicked are Satan's captives. In rejecting Christ they have accepted the rule of the rebel leader. They are ready to receive his suggestions and to do his bidding. Yet, true to his early cunning, he does not acknowledge himself to be Satan. He claims to be the prince who is the rightful owner of the world and whose inheritance has been unlawfully wrested from him. He represents himself to his deluded subjects as a redeemer, assuring them that his power has brought them forth from their graves and that he is about to rescue them from the most cruel tyranny. The presence of Christ having been removed, Satan works wonders to support his claims. He makes the weak strong and inspires all with his own spirit and energy. He proposes to lead them against the camp of the saints and to take possession of the City of God. With fiendish exultation he points to the unnumbered millions who have been raised from the dead and declares that as their leader he is well able to overthrow the city and regain his throne and his kingdom.

In that vast throng are multitudes of the long-lived race that existed before the Flood; men of lofty stature and giant intellect, who, yielding to the control of fallen angels, devoted all their skill and knowledge to the exaltation of themselves; men whose wonderful works of art led the world to idolize their genius, but whose cruelty and evil inventions, defiling the earth and defacing the image of God, caused Him to blot them from the face of His creation. There are kings and generals who conquered nations, valiant men who never lost a battle, proud, ambitious warriors whose approach made kingdoms tremble. In death these experienced no change. As they come up from the grave, they resume the current of their thoughts just where it ceased. They are actuated by the same desire to conquer that ruled them when they fell.

Satan consults with his angels, and then with these kings and conquerors and mighty men. They look upon the strength and numbers on their side, and declare that the army within the city is small in comparison with theirs, and that it can be overcome. They lay their plans to take possession of the riches and glory of the New Jerusalem. All immediately begin to prepare for battle. Skillful artisans construct implements of war. Military leaders, famed for their success, marshal the throngs of warlike men into companies and divisions.

At last the order to advance is given, and the countless host moves on—an army such as was never summoned by earthly conquerors, such as the combined forces of all ages since war began on earth could never equal. Satan, the mightiest of warriors, leads the van, and his angels unite their forces for this final struggle. Kings and warriors are in his train, and the multitudes follow in vast companies, each under its appointed leader. With military precision the serried ranks advance over the earth's broken and uneven surface to the City of God. By command of Jesus, the gates of the New Jerusalem are closed, and the armies of Satan surround the city and make ready for the onset.

Now Christ again appears to the view of His enemies. Far above the city, upon a foundation of burnished gold, is a throne, high and lifted up. Upon this throne sits the Son of God, and around Him are the subjects of His kingdom. The power and majesty of Christ no language can describe, no pen portray. The glory of the Eternal Father is enshrouding His Son. The brightness of His presence fills the City of God, and flows out beyond the gates, flooding the whole earth with its radiance.

Nearest the throne are those who were once zealous in the cause of Satan, but who, plucked as brands from the burning, have followed their Saviour with deep, intense devotion. Next are those who perfected Christian characters in the midst of falsehood and infidelity, those who honored the law of God when the Christian world declared it void, and the millions, of all ages, who were martyred for their faith. And beyond is the "great multitude, which no man could number, of all nations, and kindreds, and people, and tongues . . . before the throne, and before the Lamb, clothed with white robes, and palms in their hands" (Revelation 7:9). Their warfare is ended, their victory won. They have run the race and reached the prize. The palm branch in their hands is a symbol of their triumph, the white robe an emblem of the spotless righteousness of Christ which now is theirs.

The redeemed raise a song of praise that echoes and re-echoes through the vaults of heaven: "Salvation to our God which sitteth upon the throne, and unto the Lamb" (Revelation 7:10). And angel and seraph unite their voices in adoration. As the redeemed have beheld the power and malignity of Satan, they have seen, as never before, that no power but that of Christ could have made them conquerors. In all that shining throng there are none to ascribe salvation to themselves, as if they had prevailed by their own power and goodness. Nothing is said of what they have done or suffered; but the burden of every song, the keynote of every anthem, is: Salvation to our God and unto the Lamb.

In the presence of the assembled inhabitants of earth and heaven the final coronation of the Son of God takes place. And now, invested with supreme majesty and power, the King of kings pronounces sentence upon the rebels against His government and executes justice upon those who have transgressed His law and oppressed His people. Says the prophet of God: "I saw a great white throne, and Him that sat on it, from whose face the earth and the heaven fled away; and there was found no place for them. And I saw the dead, small and great, stand before God; and the books were opened: and another book was opened, which is the book of life: and the dead were judged out of those things which were written in the books, according to their works" (Revelation 20:11, 12).

As soon as the books of record are opened, and the eye of Jesus looks upon the wicked, they are conscious of every sin which they have ever committed. They see just where their feet diverged from the path of purity and holiness, just how far pride and rebellion have carried them in the violation of the law of God. The seductive temptations which they encouraged by indulgence in sin, the blessings perverted, the messengers of God despised, the warnings rejected, the waves of mercy beaten back by the stubborn, unrepentant heart—all appear as if written in letters of fire.

Above the throne is revealed the cross; and like a panoramic view appear the scenes of Adam's temptation and fall, and the successive steps in the great plan of redemption. The Saviour's lowly birth; His early life of simplicity and obedience; His baptism in Jordan; the fast and temptation in the wilderness; His public ministry, unfolding to men heaven's most precious blessings; the days crowded with deeds of love and mercy, the nights of prayer and watching in the solitude of the mountains; the plottings of envy, hate, and malice which repaid His benefits; the awful, mysterious agony in Gethsemane beneath the crushing weight of the sins of the whole world; His betrayal into the hands of the murderous mob; the fearful events of that night of horror—the unresisting prisoner, forsaken by His best-loved disciples, rudely hurried through the streets of Jerusalem; the Son of God exultingly displayed before Annas, arraigned in the high priest's palace, in the judgment hall of Pilate, before the cowardly and cruel Herod, mocked, insulted, tortured, and condemned to die—all are vividly portrayed.

And now before the swaying multitude are revealed the final scenes—the patient Sufferer treading the path to Calvary; the Prince of heaven hanging upon the cross; the haughty priests and the jeering rabble deriding His expiring agony; the supernatural darkness; the heaving earth, the rent rocks, the open graves, marking the moment when the world's Redeemer yielded up His life.

The awful spectacle appears just as it was. Satan, his angels, and his subjects have no power to turn from the picture of their own work. Each actor recalls the part which he performed. Herod, who slew the innocent children of Bethlehem that he might destroy the King of Israel; the base Herodias, upon whose guilty soul rests the blood of John the Baptist; the weak, timeserving Pilate; the mocking soldiers; the priests and rulers and the maddened throng who cried, "His blood be on us, and on our children!" (Matthew 27:25) —all behold the enormity of their guilt. They vainly seek to hide from the divine majesty of His countenance, outshining the glory of the sun, while the redeemed cast their crowns at the Saviour's feet, exclaiming: "He died for me!"

Amid the ransomed throng are the apostles of Christ, the heroic Paul, the ardent Peter, the loved and loving John, and their truehearted brethren, and with them the vast host of martyrs; while outside the walls, with every vile and abominable thing, are those by whom they were persecuted, imprisoned, and slain. There is Nero, that monster of cruelty and vice, beholding the joy and exaltation of those whom he once tortured, and in whose extremest anguish he found satanic delight. His mother is there to witness the result of her own work; to see how the evil stamp of character transmitted to her son, the passions encouraged and developed by her influence and example, have borne fruit in crimes that caused the world to shudder.

There are papist priests and prelates, who claimed to be Christ's ambassadors, yet employed the rack, the dungeon, and the stake to control the consciences of His people. There are the proud pontiffs who exalted themselves above God and presumed to change the law of the Most High. Those pretended fathers of the church have an account to render to God from which they would fain be excused. Too late they are made to see that the Omniscient One is jealous of His law and that He will in no wise clear the guilty. They learn now that Christ identifies His interest with that of His suffering people; and they feel the force of His own words: "Inasmuch as ye have done it unto one of the least of these My brethren, ye have done it unto Me" (Matthew 25:40).

The whole wicked world stand arraigned at the bar of God on the charge of high treason against the government of heaven. They have none to plead their cause; they are without excuse; and the sentence of eternal death is pronounced against them.

It is now evident to all that the wages of sin is not noble independence and eternal life, but slavery, ruin, and death. The wicked see what they have forfeited by their life of rebellion. The far more exceeding and eternal weight of glory was despised when offered them; but how desirable it now appears. "All this," cries the lost soul, "I might have had; but I chose to put these things far from me. Oh, strange infatuation! I have exchanged peace, happiness, and honor for wretchedness, infamy, and despair." All see that their exclusion from heaven is just. By their lives they have declared: "We will not have this Man [Jesus] to reign over us.

As if entranced, the wicked have looked upon the coronation of the Son of God. They see in His hands the tables of the divine law, the statutes which they have despised and transgressed. They witness the outburst of wonder, rapture, and adoration from the saved; and as the wave of melody sweeps over the multitudes without the city, all with one voice exclaim, "Great and marvelous are Thy works, Lord God Almighty; just and true are Thy ways, Thou King of saints" (Revelation 15:3); and, falling prostrate, they worship the Prince of life.

Satan seems paralyzed as he beholds the glory and majesty of Christ. He who was once a covering cherub remembers whence he has fallen. A shining seraph, "son of the morning;" how changed, how degraded! From the council where once he was honored, he is forever excluded. He sees another now standing near to the Father, veiling

His glory. He has seen the crown placed upon the head of Christ by an angel of lofty stature and majestic presence, and he knows that the exalted position of this angel might have been his.

Memory recalls the home of his innocence and purity, the peace and content that were his until he indulged in murmuring against God, and envy of Christ. His accusations, his rebellion, his deceptions to gain the sympathy and support of the angels, his stubborn persistence in making no effort for self-recovery when God would have granted him forgiveness —all come vividly before him. He reviews his work among men and its results—the enmity of man toward his fellow man, the terrible destruction of life, the rise and fall of kingdoms, the overturning of thrones, the long succession of tumults, conflicts, and revolutions. He recalls his constant efforts to oppose the work of Christ and to sink man lower and lower. He sees that his hellish plots have been powerless to destroy those who have put their trust in Jesus. As Satan looks upon his kingdom, the fruit of his toil, he sees only failure and ruin. He has led the multitudes to believe that the City of God would be an easy prey; but he knows that this is false. Again and again, in the progress of the great controversy, he has been defeated and compelled to yield. He knows too well the power and majesty of the Eternal.

The aim of the great rebel has ever been to justify himself and to prove the divine government responsible for the rebellion. To this end he has bent all the power of his giant intellect. He has worked deliberately and systematically, and with marvelous success, leading vast multitudes to accept his version of the great controversy which has been so long in progress. For thousands of years this chief of conspiracy has palmed off falsehood for truth. But the time has now come when the rebellion is to be finally defeated and the history and character of Satan disclosed. In his last great effort to dethrone Christ, destroy His people, and take possession of the City of God, the archdeceiver has been fully unmasked. Those who have united with him see the total failure of his cause. Christ's followers and the loyal angels behold the full extent of his machinations against the government of God. He is the object of universal abhorrence.

Satan sees that his voluntary rebellion has unfitted him for heaven. He has trained his powers to war against God; the purity, peace, and harmony of heaven would be to him supreme torture. His accusations against the mercy and justice of God are now silenced.

The reproach which he has endeavored to cast upon Jehovah rests wholly upon himself. And now Satan bows down and confesses the justice of his sentence.

"Who shall not fear Thee, O Lord, and glorify Thy name? for Thou only art holy: for all nations shall come and worship before Thee; for Thy judgments are made manifest" (Revelation 15:4). Every question of truth and error in the long-standing controversy has now been made plain. The results of rebellion, the fruits of setting aside the divine statutes, have been laid open to the view of all created intelligences. The working out of Satan's rule in contrast with the government of God has been presented to the whole universe. Satan's own works have condemned him. God's wisdom, His justice, and His goodness stand fully vindicated. It is seen that all His dealings in the great controversy have been conducted with respect to the eternal good of His people and the good of all the worlds that He has created. "All Thy works shall praise Thee, O Lord; and Thy saints shall bless Thee" (Psalm 145:10). The history of sin will stand to all eternity as a witness that with the existence of God's law is bound up the happiness of all the beings He has created. With all the facts of the great controversy in view, the whole universe, both loyal and rebellious, with one accord declare: "Just and true are Thy ways, Thou King of saints."

Before the universe has been clearly presented the great sacrifice made by the Father and the Son in man's behalf. The hour has come when Christ occupies His rightful position and is glorified above principalities and powers and every name that is named. It was for the joy that was set before Him—that He might bring many sons unto glory—that He endured the cross and despised the shame. And inconceivably great as was the sorrow and the shame, yet greater is the joy and the glory. He looks upon the redeemed, renewed in His own image, every heart bearing the perfect impress of the divine, every face reflecting the likeness of their King. He beholds in them the result of the travail of His soul, and He is satisfied. Then, in a voice that reaches the assembled multitudes of the righteous and the wicked, He declares: "Behold the purchase of My blood! For these I suffered, for these I died, that they might dwell in My presence throughout eternal ages." And the song of praise ascends from the white-robed ones about the throne: "Worthy is the Lamb that was slain to receive power, and riches, and wisdom, and strength, and honor, and glory, and blessing" (Revelation 5:12).

Notwithstanding that Satan has been constrained to acknowledge God's justice and to bow to the supremacy of Christ, his character remains unchanged. The spirit of rebellion, like a mighty torrent, again bursts forth. Filled with frenzy, he determines not to yield the great controversy. The time has come for a last desperate struggle against the King of heaven. He rushes into the midst of his subjects and endeavors to inspire them with his own fury and arouse them to instant battle. But of all the countless millions whom he has allured into rebellion, there are none now to acknowledge his supremacy. His power is at an end. The wicked are filled with the same hatred of God that inspires Satan; but they see that their case is hopeless, that they cannot prevail against Jehovah. Their rage is kindled against Satan and those who have been his agents in deception, and with the fury of demons they turn upon them.

Saith the Lord: "Because thou hast set thine heart as the heart of God; behold, therefore I will bring strangers upon thee, the terrible of the nations: and they shall draw their swords against the beauty of thy wisdom, and they shall defile thy brightness. They shall bring thee down to the pit...I will destroy thee, O covering cherub, from the midst of the stones of fire. . . . I will cast thee to the ground, I will lay thee before kings, that they may behold thee. . . . I will bring thee to ashes upon the earth in the sight of all them that behold thee. . . . Thou shalt be a terror, and never shalt thou be any more." (Ezekiel 28:6-8, 16-19).

"Every battle of the warrior is with confused noise, and garments rolled in blood; but this shall be with burning and fuel of fire... The indignation of the Lord is upon all nations, and His fury upon all their armies: He hath utterly destroyed them, He hath delivered them to the slaughter...Upon the wicked He shall rain quick burning coals, fire and brimstone and an horrible tempest: this shall be the portion of their cup" (Isaiah 9:5; 34:2; Psalm 11:6) Fire comes down from God out of heaven. The earth is broken up. The weapons concealed in its depths are drawn forth. Devouring flames burst from every yawning chasm. The very rocks are on fire. The day has come that shall burn as an oven. The elements melt with fervent heat, the earth also, and the works that are therein are burned up. Malachi 4:1; 2 Peter 3:10. The earth's surface seems one molten mass—a vast, seething lake of fire.

It is the time of the judgment and perdition of ungodly men—"the day of the Lord's vengeance, and the year of recompenses for the controversy of Zion" (Isaiah 34:8).

The wicked receive their recompense in the earth. (Proverbs 11:31). They "shall be stubble: and the day that cometh shall burn them up, saith the Lord of hosts." Malachi 4:1. Some are destroyed as in a moment, while others suffer many days. All are punished "according to their deeds." The sins of the righteous having been transferred to Satan, he is made to suffer not only for his own rebellion, but for all the sins which he has caused God's people to commit. His punishment is to be far greater than that of those whom he has deceived. After all have perished who fell by his deceptions, he is still to live and suffer on. In the cleansing flames the wicked are at last destroyed, root and branch—Satan the root, his followers the branches. The full penalty of the law has been visited; the demands of justice have been met; and heaven and earth, beholding, declare the righteousness of Jehovah.

Satan's work of ruin is forever ended. For six thousand years he has wrought his will, filling the earth with woe and causing grief throughout the universe. The whole creation has groaned and travailed together in pain. Now God's creatures are forever delivered from his presence and temptations. "The whole earth is at rest, and is quiet: they [the righteous] break forth into singing" (Isaiah 14:7). And a shout of praise and triumph ascends from the whole loyal universe. "The voice of a great multitude...as the voice of many waters, and as the voice of mighty thunderings is heard, saying: Alleluia: for the Lord God omnipotent reigneth" (Revelation 19:6).

While the earth was wrapped in the fire of destruction, the righteous abode safely in the Holy City. Upon those that had part in the first resurrection, the second death has no power. While God is to the wicked a consuming fire, He is to His people both a sun and a shield. (Revelation 20:6; Psalm 84:11).

"I saw a new heaven and a new earth: for the first heaven and the first earth were passed away" (Revelation 21:1). The fire that consumes the wicked purifies the earth. Every trace of the curse is swept away. No eternally burning hell will keep before the ransomed the fearful consequences of sin.

One reminder alone remains: Our Redeemer will ever bear the marks of His crucifixion. Upon His wounded head, upon His side,

His hands and feet, are the only traces of the cruel work that sin has wrought. Says the prophet, beholding Christ in His glory: "He had bright beams coming out of His side: and there was the hiding of His power" (Habakkuk 3:4). That pierced side whence flowed the crimson stream that reconciled man to God—there is the Saviour's glory, there the hiding of His power. Mighty to save, through the sacrifice of redemption, He was therefore strong to execute justice upon them that despised God's mercy. And the tokens of His humiliation are His highest honor; through the eternal ages the wounds of Calvary will show forth His praise and declare His power.

"O Tower of the flock, the stronghold of the daughter of Zion, unto Thee shall it come, even the first dominion" (Micah 4:8). The time has come to which holy men have looked with longing since the flaming sword barred the first pair from Eden, the time for "the redemption of the purchased possession" (Ephesians 1:14). The earth originally given to man as his kingdom, betrayed by him into the hands of Satan, and so long held by the mighty foe, has been brought back by the great plan of redemption. All that was lost by sin has been restored. "Thus saith the Lord . . . that formed the earth and made it; He hath established it, He created it not in vain, He formed it to be inhabited." Isaiah 45:18. God's original purpose in the creation of the earth is fulfilled as it is made the eternal abode of the redeemed. "The righteous shall inherit the land, and dwell therein forever" (Psalm 37:29).

A fear of making the future inheritance seem too material has led many to spiritualize away the very truths which lead us to look upon it as our home. Christ assured His disciples that He went to prepare mansions for them in the Father's house. Those who accept the teachings of God's word will not be wholly ignorant concerning the heavenly abode. And yet, "eye hath not seen, nor ear heard, neither have entered into the heart of man, the things which God hath prepared for them that love Him." 1 Corinthians 2:9. Human language is inadequate to describe the reward of the righteous. It will be known only to those who behold it. No finite mind can comprehend the glory of the Paradise of God.

In the Bible the inheritance of the saved is called "a country" (Hebrews 11:14-16). There the heavenly Shepherd leads His flock to fountains of living waters. The tree of life yields its fruit every month, and the leaves of the tree are for the service of the nations. There are ever-flowing streams, clear as crystal, and beside them waving trees cast their shadows upon the paths prepared for the ransomed of the Lord. There the wide-spreading plains swell into hills of beauty, and the mountains of God rear their lofty summits. On those peaceful plains, beside those living streams, God's people, so long pilgrims and wanderers, shall find a home. "My people shall dwell in a peaceable habitation, and in sure dwellings, and in quiet resting places... Violence shall no more be heard in thy land, wasting nor destruction within thy borders; but thou shalt call thy walls Salvation, and thy gates Praise...They shall build houses, and inhabit them; and they shall plant vineyards, and eat the fruit of them. They shall not build, and another inhabit; they shall not plant, and another eat: . . . Mine elect shall long enjoy the work of their hands" (Isaiah 32:18; 60:18; 65:21, 22).

There, "the wilderness and the solitary place shall be glad for them; and the desert shall rejoice, and blossom as the rose...Instead of the thorn shall come up the fir tree, and instead of the brier shall come up the myrtle tree..The wolf also shall dwell with the lamb, and the leopard shall lie down with the kid; . . . and a little child shall lead them...They shall not hurt nor destroy in all My holy mountain saith the Lord. (Isaiah 35:1; 55:13; 11:6, 9). Pain cannot exist in the atmosphere of heaven. There will be no more tears, no funeral trains, no badges of mourning. "There shall be no more death, neither sorrow, nor crying: . . . for the former things are passed away...The inhabitant shall not say, I am sick: the people that dwell therein shall be forgiven their iniquity" (Revelation 21:4; Isaiah 33:24).

There is the New Jerusalem, the metropolis of the glorified new earth, "a crown of glory in the hand of the Lord, and a royal diadem in the hand of thy God...Her light was like unto a stone most precious, even like a jasper stone, clear as crystal...The nations of them which are saved shall walk in the light of it: and the kings of the earth do bring their glory and honor into it...Saith the Lord: I will rejoice in Jerusalem, and joy in My people...The tabernacle of God is with men, and He will dwell with them, and they shall be His people, and God Himself shall be with them, and be their God" (Isaiah 62:3; Revelation 21:11, 24; Isaiah 65:19; Revelation 21:3).

In the City of God "there shall be no night. None will need or desire repose. There will be no weariness in doing the will of God and offering praise to His name. We shall ever feel the freshness of the morning and shall ever be far from its close. "And they need no candle, neither light of the sun; for the Lord God giveth them light" (Revelation 22:5). The light of the sun will be superseded by a radiance which is not painfully dazzling, yet which immeasurably surpasses the brightness of our noontide. The glory of God and the Lamb floods the Holy City with unfading light. The redeemed walk in the sunless glory of perpetual day.

"I saw no temple therein: for the Lord God Almighty and the Lamb are the temple of it" (Revelation 21:22). The people of God are privileged to hold open communion with the Father and the Son. "Now we see through a glass, darkly" (1 Corinthians 13:12). We behold the image of God reflected, as in a mirror, in the works of nature and in His dealings with men; but then we shall see Him face to face, without a dimming veil between. We shall stand in His presence and behold the glory of His countenance.

There the redeemed shall know, even as also they are known. The loves and sympathies which God Himself has planted in the soul shall there find truest and sweetest exercise. The pure communion with holy beings, the harmonious social life with the blessed angels and with the faithful ones of all ages who have washed their robes and made them white in the blood of the Lamb, the sacred ties that bind together "the whole family in heaven and earth" (Ephesians 3:15)— these help to constitute the happiness of the redeemed.

There, immortal minds will contemplate with never-failing delight the wonders of creative power, the mysteries of redeeming love. There will be no cruel, deceiving foe to tempt to forgetfulness of God. Every faculty will be developed, every capacity increased. The acquirement of knowledge will not weary the mind or exhaust the energies. There the grandest enterprises may be carried forward, the loftiest aspirations reached, the highest ambitions realized; and still there will arise new heights to surmount, new wonders to admire, new truths to comprehend, fresh objects to call forth the powers of mind and soul and body.

All the treasures of the universe will be open to the study of God's redeemed. Unfettered by mortality, they wing their tireless flight to worlds afar—worlds that thrilled with sorrow at the spectacle of human woe and rang with songs of gladness at the tidings of a ransomed soul. With unutterable delight the children of earth enter into the joy and the wisdom of unfallen beings. They share the treasures of knowledge and understanding gained through ages upon ages in contemplation of God's handiwork. With undimmed vision they gaze upon the glory of creation—suns and stars and systems, all in their appointed order circling the throne of Deity. Upon all things, from the least to the greatest, the Creator's name is written, and in all are the riches of His power displayed.

And the years of eternity, as they roll, will bring richer and still more glorious revelations of God and of Christ. As knowledge is progressive, so will love, reverence, and happiness increase. The more men learn of God, the greater will be their admiration of His character. As Jesus opens before them the riches of redemption and the amazing achievements in the great controversy with Satan, the hearts of the ransomed thrill with more fervent devotion, and with more rapturous joy they sweep the harps of gold; and ten thousand times ten thousand and thousands of thousands of voices unite to swell the mighty chorus of praise.

"And every creature which is in heaven, and on the earth, and under the earth, and such as are in the sea, and all that are in them, heard I saying, Blessing, and honor, and glory, and power, be unto Him that sitteth upon the throne, and unto the Lamb forever and ever" (Revelation 5:13).

The great controversy is ended. Sin and sinners are no more. The entire universe is clean. One pulse of harmony and gladness beats through the vast creation. From Him who created all, flow life and light and gladness, throughout the realms of illimitable space. From the minutest atom to the greatest world, all things, animate and inanimate, in their unshadowed beauty and perfect joy, declare that God is love.

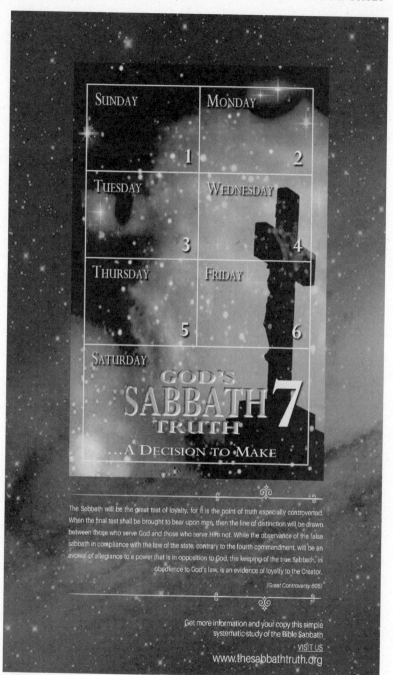

The Sabbath will be the great test of loyalty, for it is the point of truth especially controverted. When the final test shall be brought to bear upon men, then the line of distinction will be drawn between those who serve God and those who serve Him not. While the observance of the false sabbath in compliance with the law of the state, contrary to the fourth commandment, will be an avowal of allegiance to a power that is in opposition to God, the keeping of the true Sabbath, in obedience to God's law, is an evidence of loyalty to the Creator.

(Great Controversy 605)

Get more information and your copy this simple systematic study of the Bible Sabbath

VISIT US

www.thesabbathtruth.org